# First Animal
# Encyclopedia

**REVISED EDITION**
**Editor** Ishani Nandi
**Art editor** Shipra Jain
**Senior editor** Shatarupa Chaudhuri
**DTP designer** Bimlesh Tiwary
**Managing editors** Laura Gilbert,
Alka Thakur Hazarika
**Managing art editors** Diane Peyton Jones,
Romi Chakraborty
**CTS manager** Balwant Singh
**Publisher** Sarah Larter
**Senior producer, pre-production** Ben Marcus
**Producer** Nicole Landau
**Jacket editor** Laura Gilbert
**Jacket designer** Diane Peyton Jones
**Publishing director** Sophie Mitchell
**Art director** Stuart Jackman
**Consultant** John Woodward

**ORIGINAL EDITION**
**Author** Penelope Arlon
**Senior Art Editor** Tory Gordon-Harris
**Consultant** Kim Dennis-Bryan PhD. FZS
**Design Assistance** Amy McSimpson
**Publishing Manager** Sue Leonard
**Managing Art Editor** Clare Shedden
**Jacket Designer** Poppy Jenkins
**Picture Researcher** Sarah Pownall
**Production Controller** Shivani Pandey
**DTP Designer** Almudena Díaz

First American Edition, 2002
This American Edition, 2015
Published in the United States by DK Publishing
1745 Broadway, 20th Floor, New York, NY 10019

Copyright © 2002, 2015 Dorling Kindersley Limited
DK, a Division of Penguin Random House LLC
22 23 24 16 15 14
031–274454–Sept/2015

A catalog record for this title is available
from the Library of Congress.
ISBN 978-1-4654-3552-1

DK books are available at special discounts when purchased in
bulk for sales promotions, premiums, fund-raising, or educational
use. For details, contact: DK Publishing Special Markets,
1745 Broadway, 20th Floor, New York, NY 10019
SpecialSales@dk.com

Printed in China

For the curious
www.dk.com

MIX
Paper | Supporting
responsible forestry
FSC™ C018179

This book was made with Forest
Stewardship Council™ certified
paper—one small step in DK's
commitment to a sustainable future.
For more information go to
www.dk.com/our-green-pledge

# Contents

## Introduction

## Mammals

## Birds

This book will ask you questions at the bottom of each page...

## About this book

The pages of this book have special features that will show you how to get your hands on as much information as possible! Look out for these:

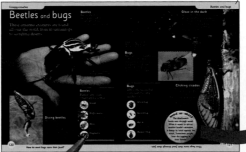

The Picture Detective quiz will get you searching through each section for the answers.

Turn and learn buttons tell you which pages to turn to in order to find more information on each subject.

Every page is colour-coded to show you which section it is in.

**weird or what?**
These buttons give extra weird and wonderful animal facts.

# The animal kingdom

The animal kingdom is divided into vertebrates and invertebrates. Mammals, birds, reptiles, amphibians, and fish are vertebrates. Insects are a type of invertebrate.

## Animals

All animals, including people, have one thing in common—they eat other living things, either plants, or animals, or both. Almost all, except a few sea creatures, can move around.

The beetle has muscles attached to its skeleton just like you do. Its skeleton is on the outside, however, while yours is on the inside.

Beetle skeleton

*Not all birds can fly, although all of them have wings.*

Bird skeleton

## What is an invertebrate?

The word invertebrate simply means not having a backbone. The "creepy-crawly" section of this book deals with the animals called invertebrates. Some of them have skeletons on the outside of their bodies, while others don't have any type of skeleton.

## What is a vertebrate?

Most of the large animals in the world are vertebrates. This means that they have a backbone, and most are made up of bones put together to make a skeleton. Mammals, birds, reptiles, amphibians, and fish are all vertebrates.

Do all animals have brains?

## Creepy-crawlies

Creepy-crawlies, or invertebrates, make up over 95 percent of all animals. But most of them are so small you don't notice them.

Stag beetle

Some people think that there are millions of creepy-crawlies we do not even know about yet.

Ants are insects, a kind of invertebrate.

Most vertebrates can move around.

## Vertebrates

All vertebrates came from the same ancestor millions of years ago, but have changed, or evolved, into these four main groups.

**Mammals:** most live on land and none can breathe underwater.

**Birds:** all birds have wings and most of them can fly.

**Fish:** all fish live in the sea or in freshwater.

**Reptiles and amphibians:** these animals live on land or in water.

The lion is one of the most ferocious meat-eaters of the mammal group.

Lions keep their sharp claws inside their toes to protect them, until they need to attack.

No, a few invertebrates have no brain.

# Mammals

You may wonder if animals such as dogs, bats, elephants, and mice have anything in common. They do—they are all mammals and have more in common than you may think.

Rodriguez flying fox

European rabbit

Orangutan

Siamese cat

Mongolian gerbil

Boxer dog

Eastern chipmunk

Red fox

Sea lion

Maned wolf

Field mice

Which mammal lives the longest?

Long-eared bats

Two-toed sloth

Pipistrelle bat

**Picture detective**
Take a look through the Mammals section and see if you can spot who these hairy skins belong to.

**Junior mammals**
Mammal babies look like little versions of their parents. They are all cared for by their mothers or both parents until they can feed and look after themselves.

Baby red-necked wallaby

Baby tiger

**Turn and learn**
The cat family:
**pp. 14-17**
Bats:
**pp. 30-31**

The Arctic bowhead whale can live to well over 100 years old.

# The world of mammals

Mammals include animals such as the whale, the kangaroo, and you and me! We all have fur, we are warm-blooded, and we feed new babies our milk.

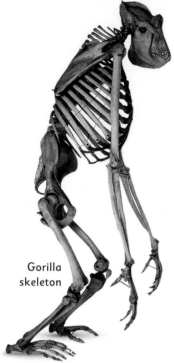

Gorilla skeleton

## The skeleton

Mammals may look very different, but stripped back to the bone, we all have the same basic bony skeleton. Scientists call us vertebrates—animals with a backbone.

## Mammal babies

Most mammal females give birth to live babies, rather than laying eggs. The baby grows inside the mother's body until it is born.

## Feeding babies

All female mammals produce milk from their bodies that they feed to their babies; this feeding is called suckling. The milk helps babies to grow.

**Turn and learn**

Bears:
**pp. 20–21**
Elephants:
**pp. 34–35**

Baby gorilla

Within the mammal group, there are many different families.

Gorillas are members of the hominid family.

How many mammal families are there?

Polar bears can live in chilly Arctic regions because they are warm-blooded and have thick fur.

## Hairy beasts

All mammals have hairy bodies, though some are much hairier than others. This hair, or fur, keeps them warm.

Elephant trunk

This elephant may not look hairy but it does have hair on its body.

## Warm blood

Mammals are warm-blooded, which means they can warm up and cool down their bodies to keep their temperature level. An elephant in the hot jungle has the same temperature as a polar bear in the snow.

Polar bears have thick fur all over their bodies.

Polar bear

## Getting around

Mammals have developed different ways of moving.

**Cats:** some mammals, such as the cat, have long legs to run with.

**Bats:** these are the only mammals that can fly—they have wings.

**Dolphins:** sea mammals have flippers and strong tails for swimming.

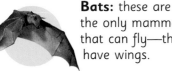

**Moles:** a mole has feet like shovels, which are useful for burrowing.

## The odd one out

It is usually true that animals give birth to live babies, but there are a few species, including this duck-billed platypus, that lay eggs. Platypus eggs are soft and the size of marbles.

There are 153 different mammal families in the world.

# Lemurs and monkeys

Monkeys and lemurs, along with the apes, make up the mammal group known as primates.

Howler monkey

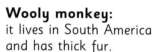
## Record breaker

Talking to each other is important to primates, which live together in large groups. The howler monkey, the loudest land animal on Earth, screams to neighboring groups. It can be heard several miles away.

Ring-tailed lemur

## Monkeys

Monkeys have grasping hands so they can climb trees. Many have recognizable features, such as this tamarin's white moustache.

The emperor tamarin has a long, white moustache.

## Lemurs

Lemurs are only found on the island of Madagascar, in the Indian Ocean. They have thin bodies and often move by jumping along on their back legs. Sitting upright with its hands on its knees, this ring-tailed lemur is sunbathing.

**weird or what?** Japanese macaques, a type of monkey, live in the mountains of northern Japan. To keep warm in the winter, they take baths in the hot volcanic springs.

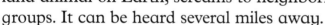

Which are longer, a monkey's arms or legs?

## Treetops
All monkeys are excellent climbers—some have long tails that they use as another limb. The spider monkey's tail is bald at the end for extra grip.

Spider monkeys have no thumbs.

Wooly spider monkey

Monkeys have long fingers for gripping branches.

Mandrill

## Ground monkey
The mandrill is one of the few monkeys that climbs trees only to sleep at night. During the day, it walks around on all fours. When a male feels threatened, it yawns widely, revealing its fearsome teeth.

Bushbaby

## Bushbaby
The bushbaby is a small primate that sleeps during the day and ventures out to hunt at night. It has huge eyes that help it to see in the dark.

A monkey's arms are longer than its legs.

# The apes

Many people confuse monkeys and apes. Apes are large, intelligent creatures that have no visible tails and can stand more upright than monkeys. You and I are members of the ape group.

## The mighty gorilla

Gorillas are the largest and most powerful of the apes, but they are rarely aggressive. They live in forests in central Africa.

## Family life

Gorillas live in groups of up to 40 animals that consist of one male and many females and babies. The males are twice the size of the females and as they mature, they grow a strip of silvery fur across their backs.

Gorilla

12

What is the dominant male gorilla in its group called?

## King of the swingers
Gibbons are the most agile of all the apes. Their wrists and shoulders are very flexible, allowing them to swing from branch to branch quickly. They live in pairs.

## Treetop apes
These orange orangutans live in the rain forests of Borneo and Sumatra up in the trees. They rarely go down to the jungle floor, preferring to eat and sleep in the treetops.

## The clever chimp
Chimpanzees are very intelligent indeed. They communicate with facial expressions and are one of the only animals to use tools.

This chimp is breaking nut shells using a piece of stone as a tool.

Grooming strengthens friendships within the group.

## Grooming
Chimps live in communities of up to 120 apes. Grooming is very important in ape societies. They can often be seen picking dirt and ticks out of each other's fur.

13

The dominant male is known as a "silverback."

# The cat family

All cats around the world spend their time doing the same sorts of activities: hunting, eating, and sleeping.

Lynx

This lynx is about twice the size of a pet cat.

## Living alone
Cats like to live on their own; only a few live in groups. Usually, the cats that live together are mothers and their babies.

## Cat carnivores
Cats only eat meat, and those living in the wild have to catch it. Some are fussier than others.

**Caracal:** these cats can leap high into the air to catch birds.

**Bobcat:** this cat lives in the woodlands of North America and eats rabbits.

**Jaguarundi:** this small, stocky cat eats anything it can catch.

**Fishing cat:** this cat catches fish by grabbing them with its claws.

Pumas are the long jumpers of the cat world. They can make massive leaps of 40 ft (12 m).

## Climbers
Some cats live in forests, and many can climb trees. They have very good balance and sharp claws that hook onto branches.

Puma

Why do cats lick their fur?

## The loudest roar
Most big cats roar; when this lion gets angry, his roar can be heard 5 miles (8 km) away! All other cats miaow, purr, and growl.

Lion

There are more than 300 million pet cats in the world. They are closely related to wild cats.

Domestic cat

## A fine coat
A cat's fur keeps it warm and camouflaged. Cats spend a lot of time licking their fur with their rough tongues to clean it.

## Cat features
All cats look similar, but their coats, shapes, and sizes are suited to where they live. This serval has a long neck and big ears to enable it to see and hear well in long grass.

## Stalk and pounce
Unlike dogs, cats cannot run fast for long distances, so most rely on their ability to stalk and pounce. When stalking, they keep their bodies low, move slowly, and then pounce.

Serval

Ocelot

### Turn and learn
Dogs that live in the wild: pp. 18-19

The ocelot is now a protected species as many were killed for their fur.

Cats lick their fur to clean themselves and to keep cool.

# Big cats

The largest, most ferocious hunters in the cat family are known as the "big cats". They include the lion, tiger, jaguar, leopard, and cheetah.

## Black leopard

Most leopards have yellow fur dotted with black spots. Black panthers were once thought to be a different type of cat, but they are actually leopards with all-black coats.

## King of the cats

Lions, found on the grassy plains of Africa, are the only cats that live in groups, or prides.

All mother cats carry their cubs in their mouths.

Pride of lions

## Sleepyheads

Cats are among the sleepiest animals in the world: they spend more than 19 hours a day asleep. Prides of lions can often be seen napping under trees. They are perfectly safe to sleep in the open, as they are in little danger of being killed by another animal.

Why do cats have whiskers?

## Water cat

The jaguar has large spots and loves swimming, which is unusual among cats. During the day it often catches fish by flipping them out of the water with its paws. At night it hunts for animals in the jungle.

Tiger

## Spotted leopard

Leopards love to climb trees. High up in the branches is a good spot to watch what is going on below. Often they will drag their kill up trees to keep it from being stolen.

Leopard

## The giant tiger

Tigers are the largest and most powerful of all the cats—they are 10 times stronger than a man! They live all over Asia, from the rain forest to the woodlands of Siberia.

Female lions do not have manes like the males.

**Turn and learn**

The fastest land mammal on Earth—the cheetah: pp. 154-155

Tigers hunt mainly in the dark.

Their whiskers help them to feel their way in the dark.

# The dog family

When you think of dogs, you probably think of pets, but many members of the dog family live in the wild.

## Wolves

Wolves live in packs of about 20, which are led by a male and female. They are meat-eaters and all work together to hunt and kill. They can grow up to 3 ft (1 m) tall and have very sharp teeth, which are useful for tearing up meat.

### Training the wolf

For thousands of years, people have trained dogs to do certain jobs.

**Guide dogs:** many dogs are used to guide blind people.

**Sheep dogs:** people have been using dogs to round up sheep for centuries.

**Police dogs:** these guard dogs are used to sniff out criminals and drugs.

European gray wolf

Wolves sometimes spray their urine to mark their territory.

At night, whole packs howl together to warn other wolves that they are there.

## Wolf language

Facial expressions and body language are used by wolves within a pack to communicate with each other. When they want to keep other wolf packs away, they howl rather than bark.

What is the tail of a fox called?

## Urban foxes

A fox is a small member of the dog family. It tends to hunt at night and lives alone or in small family groups. The red fox has become a common sight in towns and cities, where it raids trash cans for food.

Red fox

African hunting dog

When the dogs have killed, the whole pack shares the food.

These dogs are often known as "painted wolves" because of their beautiful coloring.

## Raccoon dog

This hairy dog is called the raccoon dog, although it is not related to the raccoon. It is one of the only dogs that climbs trees.

## Wild dogs

African hunting dogs live in packs of upto 30. They have long legs and lean bodies. They hunt together as a pack and can kill prey larger than themselves. They hunt at least once a day.

Gray wolves live all over the world, including in North America, northern Asia, Europe, Africa, and the Middle East.

A fox's tail is called a brush.

# Bears

Members of the bear family are big, furry mammals with large heads, thick legs, and short tails. They have five claws on each foot.

## Bear necessities

Bears have a good sense of smell, but weak eyesight and hearing. This is reflected in their large noses and very small ears and eyes.

Brown bear

## Bears of the world

There are only eight types of bear in the world, including the polar bear and the brown bear.

**Brown bear:** this big bear lives in Europe, Asia, and North America.

**Polar bear:** the biggest and most deadly bear. It lives in the Arctic.

**Spectacled bear:** it got this name because it looks as if it is wearing glasses.

## A long doze

Many bears are dormant in the winter, which means they doze or sleep nonstop during this time. They eat and eat during the summer and fall months, building up fat they can use in the winter.

The brown bear can stand up to 11 ft (3.5 m)—that's twice the height of an adult human!

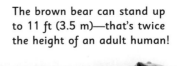

Which bear makes nests in trees?

**American black bear:** this bear sleeps up to six months during winter.

**Sloth bear:** its claws grow up to 3 in (8 cm) long, and help it tear open ant nests.

**Giant panda:** this black-and-white bear mostly lives by itself.

**Sun bear:** it uses its 10-in- (25-cm-) long tongue to suck honey out of trees.

**Asiatic black bear:** this bear has a V of white fur on its chest.

## Climbing bears

Bears normally walk slowly, but if they feel the need they can gallop at very high speeds. It may seem unlikely because of their size, but most bears are also able to climb trees. This giant panda is climbing a tree to find a safe place to rest.

The giant panda eats mostly bamboo shoots. It will sometimes eat small animals if it can find them.

## Water bears

Polar bears live in the Arctic. They have thick fur to keep them warm in the chilly weather. They are excellent swimmers and can hold their breath for up to two minutes underwater.

## Mother love

The mother bear looks after her cubs fiercely during their first year, teaching them how to survive. She sometimes stands on her back legs to increase her height and frighten enemies away.

The sun bear.

# Small and cunning

There are many small, meat-eating mammals that hunt or scavenge for their food. Many are known for their clever hunting methods.

## The weasel family
Members of the weasel family have long bodies and short legs. They have a fierce reputation for hunting—they are able to kill animals larger than themselves.

The American mink has a dark brown coat all year round.

Stoat

Weasels hunt by themselves, killing animals by biting their necks.

Weasel

## Stoats
Stoats and minks are small animals related to weasels. In summer, stoats are brown with a white tummy, and in winter, some turn white so that they are camouflaged in the snow.

### Turn and learn
The badger, a relative of the weasel:
p. 25

22

Why are many of the weasel family becoming rare?

## Raccoons

Raccoons are small animals with foxlike faces and bandit-style masks. They are inquisitive creatures who make clever hunters.

Raccoons are often seen in towns rifling through garbage. They have even been known to open door latches.

## Smelly skunks

Skunks are found in the Americas and feed on small animals and fruit. When threatened, they lift their tails and let out a foul stink, which you can smell from a half a mile away!

This mongoose has clamped its teeth around a snake's neck to kill it.

## Mongoose family

Mongooses are so cunning that they can kill some of the world's most venomous animals, such as snakes.

Meerkats

## Weasel relatives

These mammals belong to the weasel family.

**Wolverine:** this animal has a larger, stockier body than a weasel.

**Polecat:** polecats are sometimes kept as pets. They are called ferrets.

**American mink:** it hunts on land and in water.

## Meerkats

Meerkats are a type of mongoose that live in groups. They hunt during the day, while a sentry scans the area from the highest point, sitting upright, looking out for enemies.

Because many are killed for their fur.

# The burrowers

Many mammals are diggers, building their homes beneath the ground. Some use their burrows only for sleeping, while others live underground.

## Rabbits

Most rabbits dig burrows, called warrens, underground to protect themselves from enemies, to shelter from cold, and to provide a safe place for their babies. European rabbits live in large groups.

Rabbit warrens are often a maze of tunnels.

## Boxing hares

Hares are relatives of rabbits that have longer ears. They can sometimes be seen boxing during the spring breeding season. They stand on their back legs, hitting out with the front ones.

Hares do not actually live underground; they live in hollows they make with their bodies in the soil.

24

What are rabbit babies called?

## The aardvark

This animal has a body like a pig, ears like a rabbit, and it licks up ants like an anteater, but it is not related to any of these animals! It is a very good burrower, digging long tunnels with its claws.

## Armadillo

Armadillos look as if they could take on an army with their bony armored backs. They dig burrows to find food and make dens. Most rest in their burrows during the day and hunt by night.

Badgers have large, stocky bodies, and small heads with long noses to root out food.

## Badgers

Badgers have short legs that are good for scurrying down tunnels. Their burrows, known as setts, are passed down through generations of badgers. They tend to hunt at night.

Badgers have poor eyesight but a good sense of smell.

## Moles

You will know when European moles are around because they leave molehills behind on the ground. Moles spend most of their lives underground eating worms and insects.

The star-nosed mole uses its paws as paddles to "swim" through the earth.

European mole

Rabbit babies are called kittens.

# Insect-eating mammals

Many mammals spend their lives eating insects and other small creepy-crawlies. Most of them only hunt at night.

## Scaly anteater

Sometimes called a scaly anteater, this pangolin is not actually related to anteaters. It uses its long claws to dig into anthills and termite mounds.

## Giant anteater

The giant anteater is a large mammal that likes to eat ants and termites. It has a large nose and a tongue that is as long as your arm, perfect for sticking into termite mounds.

Pangolins shut their nostrils while eating ants to stop them from rushing up their noses.

## Silky anteater

The silky anteater has a shorter nose and paler fur than its cousins. It spends much of its time digging out tree ants and licking them up.

The giant anteater can eat more than 30,000 ants in one day!

**Turn and learn**

Ants and termites: **pp. 124-125** Earthworms: **p. 33**

How big is the smallest shrew?

The head and paws appear as the hedgehog sniffs its surroundings and looks out for danger.

When curled up, the hedgehog looks like a spiny ball.

## Small and prickly

Hedgehogs use their long noses to snuffle in the ground for insects and worms. They are covered in sharp spines that are made of a kind of hair. If this creature feels threatened, it rolls its body into a prickly ball. Not many animals would attempt to eat a spiny hedgehog!

The hedgehog flips itself over and goes on its way.

## Shrews

Shrews are small, active mammals that have to eat plenty of insects and worms every few hours to keep up their energy. They can eat more than their weight in food every day.

## The spiny echidna

The insect-eating echidna is also covered in spines. It is one of the most unusual animals because, with the duck-billed platypus, it is one of the only mammals that lay eggs.

Echidna

## Shrew senses

A shrew uses its very good senses of smell and hearing to find food, such as small insects and earthworms.

Pygmy shrew

The pygmy white-toothed shrew is half the size of your finger.

# Rodents

Rodents are the mammal group that includes mice and rats. Rodents are found all over the world, from deserts to the Arctic.

A rat's tail helps it to balance and turn in the water.

## The brown rat

The rat is considered a pest. It lives almost everywhere in the world and can exist in huge numbers if enough food is available.

Brown rat

## Dinnertime

Rats eat everything we eat and more, which is why they can survive worldwide. The brown rat is a very good swimmer and can catch small fish underwater.

Rats and mice have a very good sense of smell and "talk" to each other using their body smells.

### weird or what?

The black rat was responsible for killing half the population of London in 1665. It brought fleas to England that carried a deadly disease called the bubonic plague.

## Rodent teeth

All rodents have four big front teeth, like this marmot's. They are very sharp.

What is the biggest rodent in the world?

## Rodent groups

Over 40 percent of the world's mammals are rodents. They come in many shapes and sizes.

**Hamster:** this creature comes from Western Asia and is a very popular pet.

**Squirrel:** it is an excellent tree climber and uses its tail for balance.

**Vole:** water voles live by rivers and lakes and make burrows in the banks.

**Naked mole rat:** it lives underground and burrows with its teeth.

**Porcupine:** this animal has sharp quills that it raises when threatened.

## Mice

Mice have pointed noses and long whiskers, which help them find their way around dark corners. This house mouse eats many different types of food and can produce 36,000 droppings in a year.

Harvest mice use their tails like hands, to grip onto stalks.

Harvest mouse

House mouse

## Towns of rodents

Some rodents live on their own, but these North American prairie dogs live in large underground communities called towns. Each town comprises a number of burrows connected by long tunnels.

## A long, long sleep

The dormouse can be found in the woods and fields of Europe and is an excellent climber and jumper. It hibernates, or sleeps, for seven months during the winter without waking.

# Flying mammals

Some mammals have "wings," so they can glide through the air, but bats are the only mammals that can actually fly by flapping their wings.

Flying squirrel

Greater mouse-eared bats

During the day, bats roost in dark caves, trees, or under a roof of a building. They sleep upside-down.

## The glider

The flying squirrel has big flaps of skin on either side of its body. When it jumps, it opens them out like an umbrella and can glide for 330 ft (100 m), steering with its tail and legs.

## Bats

Bats' wings are actually long arms with skin stretching between each finger. Their thumbs stick out like small claws to grip branches.

Clawlike thumb

Bats squeak to find one another in the dark.

Vampire bat

The saliva of the vampire bat numbs the skin of its victim so it can't feel the bloodsucking bite.

## The real vampire

The vampire bat's favorite meal is fresh blood, even yours! It feeds by digging its sharp teeth into the flesh, then laps up the blood.

## Bat features

A bat's head shape reflects the way it feeds.

**Fruit bat:** has a long snout and a long tongue to sip nectar and eat fruit.

**Long-eared bat:** this bat has large ears that can hear insects' wings flapping.

**Long-nosed bat:** these bats have long noses to help them smell flowers.

What is the smallest bat in the world?

## Bat babies

Some bats bring up their babies together in a huge nursery, often filled with thousands of bats. Amazingly the mother can always find her baby when she returns with food.

Fruit bat

## Bat diet

Most bats eat insects. Others, like this fruit bat, use their long tongues to eat fruit and sip nectar from flowers.

## Catching insects

Bats are very good at catching insects in midair—in the dark! They find them by making clicking noises and listening for the echoes bouncing off insects.

### Turn and learn

Gliding frogs:
**pp. 100–101**
Bloodsuckers:
**pp. 116–117**

This Geoffroy's long-nosed bat drinks nectar.

The Kitti's hog-nosed bat is the smallest—it is the size of a bumble bee.

# Marsupials

A marsupial is a mammal with a pocket, called a pouch, for carrying its babies.

## More marsupials

Except for a few that live in South America, almost all marsupials come from Australasia. They vary a lot in looks.

**Dorian's tree kangaroo:** this small kangaroo can climb trees.

**Numbat:** this marsupial feeds almost entirely on antlike termites.

**Rabbit-eared bandicoot:** These large-eared burrowers are most active at night.

## Koala

Koalas look like little bears. They live in Australia and are the only animals that eat eucalyptus leaves. The leaves are so hard to digest that koalas spend 19 hours a day sleeping while their stomachs settle.

## Little devil

The Tasmanian devil is not much bigger than a small dog, but it is very aggressive. It is the biggest meat-eating marsupial and has such powerful jaws that it can eat an entire animal—bones and all!

A kangaroo's front legs are

## Bouncing marsupials

Kangaroos cannot walk. Instead, they have enormous back legs that they use to jump everywhere. They can move very fast just by leaping.

**Turn and learn**

A mammal that lays eggs: p. 9 and p. 27

Which are bigger, wallabies or kangaroos?

## Supermum!

Opossums live in the Americas. Unusually for marsupials, the mother has no pouch. Instead, her babies cling to her. Sometimes one mother can have upto 20 babies at one time!

Opossums are very good tree climbers.

The joey belonging to this mother is definitely big enough to climb out of its pouch.

## In the pouch

Most marsupials have pouches. When the babies are born, they are as small as beans and wriggle straight into the pouch. They do most of their growing there, instead of inside their mothers.

## Little joey

Kangaroo and wallaby babies are commonly known as joeys. They spend several months in the mother's pouch, and even when they are big enough to walk, they sometimes jump back in for safety.

not used when it hops.

Their huge tails help to balance them when they hop.

33

# The mighty elephants

Elephants are the largest land animals on Earth—the biggest one ever found weighed as much as 150 men! There are two main types of elephant: the African and the Asian.

African elephants flap their enormous ears to keep themselves cool in the hot sun.

African elephants

## Living in herds

African elephants live in groups called herds. However, only females and youngsters live together; males live on their own. A family usually contains about eight to 10 elephants.

Elephants' tusks are very big upper teeth.

## Playtime!

Baby elephants love to play, which is an important part of growing up in a herd. They chase one another, throw sticks, and climb all over each other.

How big is an elephant's toenail?

## An amazing nose

Elephants have enormous noses, called trunks. But they are no ordinary noses—they do many more jobs than simply smelling. Elephants use their trunks to eat, drink, wash, and even pick up vibrations from the ground.

Elephants make loud, trumpeting calls to each other.

Asian elephant

Elephants use their trunks to grab leaves high up in the trees that other animals cannot reach.

## A handy nose

An elephant can grip things with the end of its nose, like people do with their hands. It uses its trunk to grasp plants and eat them, to greet other elephants, and to show aggression to others.

## Bathtime!

An elephant's skin is sensitive and needs to be washed regularly to rinse away creepy-crawlies and keep it cool. An elephant sucks up water in its trunk and sprays it over its body.

African elephants have much bigger ears than Asian elephants.

An elephant's toenail is as big as your hand!

35

# Hoofed mammals

A hoof is a certain type of foot with a hard covering. Hoofed mammals are found all over the world.

## Different hoofs

A hoofed foot has a hard case, like a big toenail, around each toe for strength. Hoofed feet are good for running fast.

**Horse:** a horse has only one toe surrounded by a hoof. It runs on tiptoe.

**Rhinoceros:** these large-hoofed mammals have three toes.

**Camel:** the camel has two toes that are widely spaced for walking on sand.

## Wild pigs

Pigs are hoofed mammals that eat almost anything. Wild pigs are speedy runners and protective of their little, striped babies.

## The tapir

Tapirs have very long noses and look like pigs, but they belong to a different hoofed family.

## On bended knee

The warthog is a long-legged African pig. When it feeds, it kneels on its wrists.

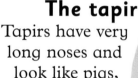

## Quick, duck!

Tapirs spend much of their time in the water. When threatened, they sink in the water, leaving their noses poking above the surface like a snorkel so they can breathe.

The nose and upper lip form a trunk.

Malaysian tapir

What is the tallest hoofed mammal?

## Deer of the north

Reindeer (also called caribou) live in cold northern parts of the world. Twice a year they "migrate"—take a long journey—for thousands of miles to avoid bad weather and to breed.

## Deer giants

The elk (also known as moose) lives in northern swampy forests. It is the largest deer in the world. Its antlers can grow to 7 ft (2 m) across—bigger than an umbrella—with up to 20 spikes on them.

Deer lose their antlers and grow new ones every year.

## Deer

Deer are woodland animals that live together in small groups, called herds. They have antlers, which are made of bone.

## Branching out

Only male deer have antlers (except for female caribou, which also have them). Deer antlers are always branched, unlike the pointed horns of cattle.

37

The giraffe, which can be up to 20 ft (6 m) tall.

# The cattle family

Cattle are hoofed mammals. They are herbivores, which means they eat plants. They have four stomachs to digest the plants they eat.

### Early walkers

Many members of the cattle family are killed for food by other animals. Babies, like this wildebeest calf, are able to run within hours of their birth, so they can try to stay out of danger.

### Grazers and browsers

All members of the cattle family eat plants. Some are grazers, who eat low grass. Others, such as this gerenuk, are browsers: they eat from trees and shrubs.

### The herd

Most wild cattle live in large herds for safety. These bison move around together, according to the seasons and the available food.

Do members of the cattle family lose their horns yearly like deer?

## The horn collection

Unlike deer, members of the cattle family do not have branched horns.

**Antelope:** male antelopes have long, pointed horns.

**Bighorn sheep:** the horns of the male sheep curve almost in a circle.

**Blackbuck:** these impressive horns are long and wiggly.

**Muskox:** their horns curve all the way down, then up at the tips.

**Ibex:** this mountain goat has huge, thick horns that curve over its back.

**Sitatunga:** male sitatungas have long spiral horns.

## Wild sheep

Like farmed sheep, wild sheep are good at living in rocky regions.

Barbary sheep

## Spring in its step

The springbok gets its name from its high springlike bounces that show predators— animals that want to eat it—how quick it is.

## Taming the beast

Wild cows, sheep, and goats were tamed thousands of years ago to provide meat, milk, and leather for humans. Domestic cows are distant relatives of wild cattle.

Jersey cow

No, cattle keep their horns for life.

# The horse family

Thousands of years ago, horses were wild animals. Later, humans tamed them, and wild horses almost disappeared. Zebras are some of the only wild horses left.

### The hoof

All horses have one toe on each foot surrounded by a hoof. They run on tiptoe, which means they can run very fast. All horses have long tails and manes.

Stallion

Male horses are called stallions, and females are called mares.

The hard hoof protects the toe.

### Mustangs

The wild horses in the US are actually tame horses that escaped into the wild hundreds of years ago. They live in herds of one male and lots of females.

How does a horse scratch its back?

## Mood swings

Horses communicate with each other by moving their heads, tails, and ears.

**Teeth showing:** horses bare their teeth when they are unhappy or if they are sniffing the air.

**Ears back:** when a horse is angry, it puts its ears back flat against its head.

**Ears forward:** when a horse is paying attention, it has its ears facing forward.

## The wild ones

Wild members of the horse family are smaller than most tame horses, and they have longer ears. Donkeys were previously wild, but were domesticated long ago. The kiang and onager are wild breeds that live in Asia.

## Striped horses

Zebras are striped horses. No one knows why they are striped, but we do know that, like our fingerprints, each zebra's stripes are unique. They live in Africa in large herds and graze on grass.

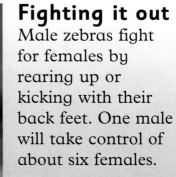

## Fighting it out

Male zebras fight for females by rearing up or kicking with their back feet. One male will take control of about six females.

Plains zebras

A horse likes to scratch its back by rolling around on the ground.

# Hoofed giants

The last group of hoofed mammals are by no means the least. They are some of the biggest animals in the world. Meet the hoofed giants.

## Smaller relatives

Some cousins of the hoofed giants are much smaller in size.

**Okapi:** this animal is the only relative of the giraffe. It has a much shorter neck.

**Pygmy hippo:** this small hippo is a fifth the size of its cousin.

**Alpaca:** alpacas and llamas are camel cousins that live in South America.

## Healthy appetite

Giraffes are never short of food—they have such long necks that they can reach high leaves on trees.

## Giraffes

The giraffe is the world's tallest animal. It is taller than three tall men standing on each other's heads!

How much can a camel drink at one time?

A two-humped camel is called a bactrian.

## The huge rhinoceros

The rhinoceros has skin that is thicker than this book and huge horns that are made of hair.

White rhino

## Ships of the desert

Camels live in hot, dry places. Their humps act like huge food stores of fat that they can use when there is nothing available to eat.

## The hippopotamus

This mammal giant has a huge, stocky body and stumpy legs. It spends a lot of time in water and it is so heavy it can walk along the bottom of a lake without floating. A hippo can hold its breath for five minutes.

Indian rhino

There are very few rhinos left because people kill them for their horns.

Giraffes are so tall, they have to spread their front legs out wide to be able to bend low enough to reach the water.

A camel can drink nine buckets of water without stopping.

# Water mammals

Not all mammals live on land—some live in water. Unlike fish, however, water mammals have to go to the surface to breathe.

### Seals

Seals, which include sea lions and walruses, have flippers instead of arms and legs. These make them very good at swimming but not good at walking.

**Turn and learn**

Giant mammals of the sea: **pp. 46-47**

Sea lions can walk more easily than other seals because their flippers are able to move in several directions.

### Underwater lives

Seals spend most of their lives in water, but return to land to have babies. They have a thick layer of fat, called blubber, which keeps them warm.

Seals are often very playful in the water.

44

What noise do seals make?

## Otters

Otters are mammals that have webbed feet to help them swim. The river otter lives along riverbanks and spends its days swimming to catch food.

### Otters of the sea

The sea otter is the smallest sea mammal. It has luxurious, thick fur that keeps it very warm. It rarely comes to land, and even sleeps in the water. When it nods off, it wraps itself up in kelp plants to stop it from drifting away!

### Sea cows

Manatees are often called sea cows because they are so big and they "graze" on underwater plants. They spend all their lives in water, and even give birth there.

Walruses use their noses, like pigs, to root around the seafloor for food, such as crabs or sea urchins.

### Walruses

Walruses are huge sea mammals. They have powerful, blubbery bodies and two large, front teeth, called tusks, which can grow up to 3 ft (1 m) long. Their tusks help them cut through ice sheets and keep enemies away.

### In the pink

Walruses are normally grayish brown in color. But when they sunbathe, they turn blush-pink because their blood rushes to the surface of their skin to cool it down.

Seals bark like dogs!

# Ocean giants

Whales and dolphins look like fish but they are actually mammals. The whales include the biggest animals that have ever lived.

## The big blue
The blue whale is the largest animal in the world—its heart is the size of a small car. The next largest creature, a bull African elephant, could sit on its tongue!

## Toothed whales
There are two kinds of whales—toothed whales and baleen whales. Toothed whales eat fish and large animals, such as seals. The killer whale can even leap onto beaches to grab unfortunate seals.

## Baleen whales
Some whales, such as this humpback, have bristly filters called baleen plates instead of teeth. These are called baleen whales. They gulp huge amounts of water, then sift it through the plates to remove the food—tiny animals called plankton.

**Turn and learn**
Water mammals: **pp. 44–45**
Plankton: **pp. 140–141**

What animal makes the loudest noise on Earth?

# Underwater gossip

Whales live in groups, or pods, and many talk to each other using squeaks, whistles, rumbles, or clicks. Beluga whales "speak" so much that they are sometimes called sea canaries.

## Whales

Most whales look very similar, but a few have different features.

**Narwhal:** this whale has an enormous swordlike tusk, which is actually a tooth.

**Porpoise:** the porpoise is a toothed whale that looks similar to a dolphin.

**Sperm whale:** this whale holds the record for the deepest dive of any mammal.

**Amazon River dolphin:** this dolphin is one of the only freshwater whales.

# Leaping dolphins

Dolphins are small whales. They are highly intelligent and curious, and they are often seen leaping alongside boats at sea.

Bottlenose dolphin

Dolphins have very strong tails that help them leap high above the surface.

Dolphins leap out of the water to avoid enemies—leaping helps them to swim faster—and to herd fish by making loud splashes.

# Underwater babies

Whale and dolphin babies, called calves, grow inside their mothers, like other mammals. The calf drinks its mother's milk until it is old enough to eat solid food. Spotted dolphins, like this mother and calf, live in groups of up to 15.

Spotted dolphin

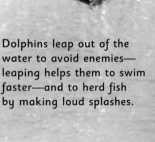

The blue whale is the loudest animal—it makes a very deep rumble.

# Birds

Most birds can fly. Thanks to this ability, they have been able to live in places that other animals could not reach. Birds live all over the world, even in the chilly Arctic.

Pigeon

Scientists have discovered that modern birds evolved from dinosaurs.

Toucan

Finches

Budgerigars

Parrot

Doves

Owl

Hummingbird

Stork

Ostrich

Penguin

Duck

Kiwi

Avocet

Which bird has the most feathers?

**Buzzard**

## Picture detective
Take a look through the bird pages and see if you can spot whose body parts these are.

Bush-robin

Blackbird

Parakeets

Macaw

## A world full of birds
There are almost 10,000 different kinds of bird in the world. They range from the enormous, flightless ostrich, which is taller than a man, to the bee hummingbird, which is smaller than your thumb.

Flamingo

Turkey

Chicken

### Turn and learn
Flying mammals:
**pp. 30-31**
Flying insects:
**pp. 110-111**

The whistling swan—it has roughly 25,000!

# The world of birds

Only a few animals in the world are able to fly—insects, bats, and birds. But none of them are more powerful or skilled than birds.

Birds spend much of their time looking after, or preening, their feathers to keep them in good condition.

Feathers are made up of tiny hairlike barbs that all mesh together.

## Feathered friends

Birds are the only creatures that have feathers. They use them to fly and to keep warm. Some birds use brightly colored feathers for display.

A rigid "backbone," or quill, runs through the center of the wing feathers, strengthening them for flying.

## Feathers

Different feathers have different jobs on a bird.

**Outer wing:** strong feathers to provide power in flight.

**Inner wing:** has smooth and flat feathers to help in flight.

**Tail feather:** long and thin for steering and balancing during flight.

**Body feather:** soft and downy to keep a bird warm. Some are exotic colors.

### Turn and learn
Nest-making: **pp. 54-55**
Exotic birds: **pp. 72-73**

50

What is the world's smallest bird?

# Flight

Birds that can fly have wings and very light skeletons—many of the bones are hollow. Their short and compact bodies also help make them neat fliers.

By flapping its wings up and down, the bird remains in the air.

Red-tailed minla

There are two methods of flying; flapping, like this red-tailed minla, and gliding.

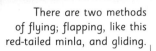

## Traveling birds

About one-third of birds spend summer in one place, then when winter sets in they fly thousands of miles to a warmer spot. Often they go to exactly the same places year after year.

## Feet

The shapes of birds' feet vary in different habitats.

**Eagle foot:** birds of prey have sharp talons to kill and grip animals.

**Perching foot:** songbirds have three toes in front and one behind for perching.

**Webbed foot:** waterfowl have webbed feet to help them paddle on water.

**Ostrich foot:** two thick toes help this flightless bird to run very fast.

## Bills

The shape and size of a bird's bill, or beak, show what it eats.

**Duck:** wide and flat to tear plants and filter food underwater.

**Woodpecker:** long and hard to chisel into wood and pick out insects.

**Chaffinch:** short and cone-shaped, ideal for cracking seeds.

**Heron:** ideal for stabbing fish underwater.

## Communication

All birds have good hearing so they can respond to songs from other members of their family. Birds are known for their tunes, and some, like this parrot, even speak.

The smallest bird in the world is the bee hummingbird.

# Courtship

At various stages in her life, a female bird will be on the lookout for a mate. Males go out of their way to impress the ladies, often in spectacular ways.

## Fierce competition

There is often competition between the males to attract the females, so performances have to be very slick. This female has chosen her mate.

Crowned cranes

## A good decorator

The male satin bowerbird builds an avenue of twigs, and at each end he places a collection of anything he finds attractive, such as shells, bones, or berries. The female picks the bower she finds the most appealing.

**weird but true**
Some birds of prey perform amazing aerobatic displays. The male and female lock talons in midair and fall almost to the ground before swooping up again.

In which season do birds start courting?

## Pairing off
It is important for birds to find the right partner.

**Peacock:** the male shows off by shaking his spectacular tail.

**Swans:** when a male and female swan mate, they stay together for life.

**Pheasant:** male pheasants fight aggressively with each other for females.

## Building a home
The male weaver bird builds an incredible nest that hangs from a branch. When a female passes by, he hangs beneath it fluttering his golden wings and shrieking to her to join him.

Spotted-backed weaver

## Foot dance
The blue-footed booby has blue feet, which attracts the females. When a male wants a mate, he dances and lifts his feet to show them off.

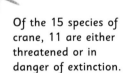

Once cranes have selected a partner they dance together, then bow, leap, bounce, and make sudden frantic runs.

Of the 15 species of crane, 11 are either threatened or in danger of extinction.

## Show off
The male frigate bird has a huge, red neck pouch, which he inflates with air when he is looking for a mate. When a female passes by, he wobbles it around and makes gobbling noises to impress her.

Birds mostly court each other in the spring.

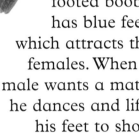

# Nesting

All birds lay eggs, which other animals find tasty. To keep their eggs safe, many birds build nests.

## A city in a nest

Some weavers, called social weavers, build one huge nest to hold lots of birds. This only happens in dry regions, because if it got too heavy with rain it would fall.

Hummingbirds are the smallest birds in the world.

Weaver bird

## Out of reach

The most important thing about a nest is that no enemies can reach it. For this reason many birds build their nests in trees.

Weaver birds go one step further than building nests in trees; they build them hanging down from branches.

## Tiny home

This hummingbird has built its nest on a fir cone. Some hummingbirds use spiders' webs to secure their nests.

Which birds are able to tie knots?

## Nests

Some birds go to great lengths to make amazing-looking nests.

**Tunnel home:** some weaver birds build nests with tunnel entrances.

**In the reeds:** the reed warbler builds its nest between thin reeds.

**Mud nest:** the domed ovenbird makes its nest entirely out of mud.

**Tree trunk:** A blue tit has built this nest in a hollow tree trunk.

## A perfect fit

Round, hollow nests like this are called cup nests. Birds build them in trees using twigs, feathers, moss, and anything else they can find.

When a bird has made its nest, it turns around and around in it until it has made a perfect hollow.

## Handy holes

Hollowed-out trees are good places to keep eggs safe. Woodpeckers make nests by chiseling through the wood with their sharp beaks. The following year, birds such as parrots may use it.

Pileated woodpecker

## Ground eggs

Some birds don't make nests at all. Instead, they lay their eggs on the ground. These Eurasian oystercatchers' eggs are camouflaged against the pebbles.

## Safety in numbers

Along the west coast of Africa, thousands of cape gannets lay their eggs at the same time right next to each other. This reduces the chance of the eggs being eaten.

The eggs are speckled and difficult to spot.

## Eggs

Birds' eggs come in a variety of sizes and colors.

Southern cassowary egg

# Hatching out

Making or finding a nest is a lot of work for birds, but caring for the eggs and chicks is even harder!

Inside the eggs, each chick grows using the yolk as food.

## Helpless nestlings

The mother bird sits on her nest keeping the eggs warm until they hatch. When they are born, they need constant feeding until they can look after themselves.

Blue tit chicks

At one day old, the bald chicks are very hungry.

At three days old, the chicks are demanding constant food. Their bright mouths are easily seen by parents.

After two weeks, there is barely enough room to move. The chicks are now ready to fly away.

At nine days, their feathers are starting to appear and the nest is getting crowded.

## Baby birds

There are two types of young bird. Some are born blind and naked and depend completely on their parents. The other type, like ducklings, hatch with open eyes and a coat of downy feathers.

## Waterbirds

Waterbirds are often born on the ground rather than in nests, so they have to be able to get out of danger quickly. Ducklings take to water very soon after hatching.

Duckling

The chick has an egg tooth that it uses to poke through the shell.

It then pushes against both ends and breaks itself out of the egg.

Egg tooth

Which bird builds the biggest nests in the world?

# Swan family

A female swan lays up to eight eggs in a clutch and only she looks after them. When the chicks are born, both parents take care of them for about five months.

These swan chicks catch a ride on their mother's back.

Wren

# Feeding frenzy

Both parents may feed their chicks. Some make up to 1,000 trips a day between them to bring enough food back to the nest.

# Rotten parents

Cuckoos don't look after their chicks. Instead, the female lays her egg in another bird's nest. When it hatches, the chick kicks out the other eggs.

The cuckoo chick is fed by the adopted parents and is often bigger than they are.

The bald eagle.

# Songbirds

Most of the world's birds are part of a huge group known as the songbirds. They spend a lot of their time in flight.

## A variety of birds
Members of the songbird group vary in looks, habits, and songs.

**Robin:** European robins are easy to spot because of their red bellies.

**Blackbird:** the blackbird often sings in the evenings from a high perch.

**Warbler:** these birds are known for their different songs, including a scolding song.

## Foot perch
Songbirds, or perchers, all have a unique type of foot, which helps them to grip onto even the thinnest branches. Three of their toes point forward and one points backward.

The short beak is used to crack hard foods, such as nutshells.

Songbirds can sleep on twigs and branches without falling off.

Blue tit

## Finding food
Like this song thrush, most songbirds are small, but because they use up a lot of energy flying, they need a lot of food. Thrushes feed on fruit, insects, worms, and snails.

How do songbirds learn how to sing?

Songbird parents feed their chicks
until they are 10 to 15 days old.

## Bird songs

Each species of songbird has its
own special song, using different
notes and rhythms. Most of the
singing is performed by males.

## Dawn chorus

Male songbirds sing loudly at
dawn to claim their nesting
territories and attract females.
Somehow, the females can hear
and identify the correct tune
among the many melodies.

### weird or what?

The Australian
lyrebird cannot only
imitate other birds' songs
but also other sounds
it hears in the rain forest,
such as chainsaws and
even camera clicks!

## Safety in flocks

Many songbirds live in
groups, called flocks. They
collect food together and join
forces to fight off bigger birds
that might eat them.

Many songbirds are
small and compact,
with short beaks.

Dunnock

By listening to sounds the male parent makes and copying them.

# Life in the air

Some birds are spectacular acrobats. They are the experts of the air—a few can even fly backward! Many birds spend most of their lives in the air.

Hummingbirds have long beaks that they poke into flowers to sip the nectar.

## Hummingbirds
These tiny birds beat their wings in a figure-eight pattern. This means that they can hover and fly backward! Smaller species beat their wings 80 times a second.

Magenta-throated woodstar hummingbird

## Record holder
The smallest bird in the world is the bee hummingbird. Found in Cuba, it feeds on nectar from flowers. Its eggs are smaller than peas!

Bee hummingbird

Some flying insects are bigger than the bee hummingbird.

## Air acrobats
Swifts, swallows, and martins are some of the most agile fliers in the bird world. They can catch insects while they are flying and even swoop down over water, like this swallow, and drink without landing.

Swallow

What is unusual about the sword-billed hummingbird?

## Nesting
Swifts, such as this chimney swift, spend a lot of their time in the air, but they must land when they are ready to nest.

## Swallows' nests
Swallows collect mud pellets and mold them into cup-shaped nests. These can often be seen beneath the eaves of buildings. The parents feed the chicks by hovering near them rather than landing.

Swallows have small beaks, but big mouths to catch insects in midair.

Forked tail

**Turn and learn**
Other nesting methods:
**pp. 54-55**

Other nesting methods:
**pp. 54-55**

## Nesting in burrows
Sand martins look similar to swallows. They make their nests by digging burrows in soft ground along riverbanks or in cliffs.

## Flying high
Swifts can spend months in the air without landing. They even sleep on the wing!

Swift

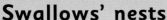

It is the only bird whose beak is longer than its body.

61

# Freshwater birds

If you search around fresh water anywhere in the world, you will find teams of birds living on it or near it. Some are swimmers and others are waders.

The male mallard makes a lower pitched quack than the female, and whistles as well.

Swan

Geese

Mallard duck (female)

Cygnets (baby swans)

Mallard drake (male)

## Kingfishers

Kingfishers live by rivers. They perch on branches above the water waiting for fish to swim past. When they see one, they dive!

## Waterfowl

Ducks, geese, and swans are waterfowl. They have boat-shaped bodies and webbed feet, which make them very good swimmers.

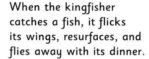

When the kingfisher catches a fish, it flicks its wings, resurfaces, and flies away with its dinner.

## Bottoms up!

Waterfowl have long bills with sharp ridges along them to grip slippery fish. Mallards often feed by tipping their heads into the water to reach plants.

62

Flamingo

Black-
crowned
night heron

Wattled
jacana

This stork, with
its hunchback and
bald neck, is often
described as ugly.

Heron

Marabou
stork

## Waders

Waders have long legs that allow
them to walk in shallow water
without getting their feathers
wet. Some also have long necks
for reaching down to food.

## Have a stab

Herons are found living
next to rivers and lakes. They eat
fish, which they catch by darting
their "s"-shaped necks forwards
at lightning speed and stabbing
the fish with their sharp beaks.

## Pink flamingos

Flamingos live in huge flocks, of
sometimes a million birds! Many
of them are pink because of the
tiny shrimps that they eat.

Flamingos
sleep in
the water,
often on
one leg.

Flamingo

Flamingos' bills act like
sieves to filter out tiny
food from the water.

### Turn
and learn

Migrating birds:
**pp. 76–77**
Sea birds:
**pp. 64–65**

Herons can live up to 20 years.

# Sea birds

## A life at sea
A lot of sea birds, such as this albatross, have webbed feet that help them swim, and special beaks to hold slippery fish.

Many birds spend their lives next to the sea or out on the open ocean. Some return to land only to breed and raise young.

Webbed feet

An albatross can glide for hours without flapping its wings.

## Dramatic divers
The sea is full of prey and birds have various ways to catch it. Some chase fish underwater while others, such as gannets and boobies, dive like torpedoes from the air to snatch them.

## Other sea birds
The coastlines of the world are always packed with sea birds.

**Herring gull:** this bird is common in Europe and North America.

**Inca tern:** this bright-beaked bird lives on the west coast of South America.

**Cormorant:** this bird can also be found inland in Europe, Asia, and Africa.

Pelican

Pelicans also use their large mouths to catch rainwater for drinking.

## A mouthful of fish
A pelican dives underwater and scoops up fish in its large mouth. It can fit three times more fish in its mouth pouch than in its stomach!

How long can birds survive without returning to land?

## Cliff birds

These black-legged kittiwakes, like many sea birds, live in huge, noisy groups on cliff faces. They even nest and lay their eggs on the narrow ledges.

Kittiwakes

The cliffs are a safe place to rest, away from enemies.

The albatross' beak is hooked, with special ridges to help it hold onto fish.

## A flock of gulls

Gulls can often be seen in huge numbers along the seashore. They eat almost anything, raiding garbage dumps and stealing other birds' eggs.

## Puffins

A puffin has webbed feet and small wings, which it uses like fins to swim, as well as to fly. It raises its one chick, called a puffling, in a burrow.

The puffin can dive to depths of 200 ft (60 m).

Puffin

### Turn and learn

The ultimate sea bird—the penguin: pp. 66-67

## What a lot of fish!

Atlantic puffins have large, colorful beaks. The top bill and tongue are ridged with spikes that enable it to hold lots of fish at once.

Some do not return to land for five years!

# In the chill

You have to be pretty tough to survive the freezing temperatures of the Antarctic. But some birds not only survive but thrive in the chill.

## Penguins

Most penguins, such as these emperor penguins, live in colonies, which can consist of hundreds of thousands of birds.

Penguins cannot fly but they sometimes leap into the water from icebergs.

## Water wings

Penguins may look clumsy on land and can't even make it into the air, but in the water they are master swimmers. They use their wings as flippers and their tails and feet to steer.

## Keeping warm

To keep them warm in icy water and in the snow, penguins have a dense covering of waterproof feathers and many layers of fat.

Egg

How long can a penguin stay underwater?

## Other snow birds

One of the few birds that lives and breeds on Antarctica all year round is the snow petrel. It is completely white, which keeps it hidden in the snow.

Penguins' feet are positioned so far back that when they stand upright, they have to use their tails to balance or they would topple over backward.

Antarctic skua

## Penguin predators

This Antarctic skua lives on or near the ice in Antarctica and nests at the coast. It eats penguin eggs and even baby penguins if they are left unguarded.

Adult penguins have white tummies and dark backs, which help to camouflage them in the water.

## Penguin parents

King penguins tuck their eggs under their bellies, resting them on their feet. The parents take turns looking after their egg. When king penguin chicks are born, they are covered in brown, downy feathers.

**Turn and learn**
Flightless birds: **pp. 78-79**
Other sea birds: **pp. 64-65**

In very cold conditions chicks and penguins huddle together for warmth.

## Slip-sliding around

Penguins find it hard to walk, so they often slide on their bellies over snow and ice, pushing with their flippers and feet.

The chicks must be fed until they grow adult, waterproof feathers

The emperor penguin holds the record for the longest time underwater—20 minutes.

67

# Birds of prey

With their sharp sight, strong talons, and hooked beaks, birds of prey are the hunting kings of the bird world.

## Hunting

Many birds of prey spot an animal on the ground from very high up in the air with their excellent eyesight. They swoop down and grab it with their sharp talons.

African hawk eagle

Birds of prey are the only birds that kill with their feet.

Secretary bird

These birds are famous for eating snakes, which they kill by stamping on them.

Eagles are the most powerful of the birds of prey. They can kill animals as big as themselves.

## Stepping out

Secretary birds have incredibly longs legs. They rarely fly. Instead they can be seen taking long strides across the grasslands of Africa.

Which is the fastest bird of prey?

Red tailed buzzard

A buzzard's wings are huge, which means they are fast flyers that can glide and even hover without flapping their wings.

## The vulture
Vultures are the waste collectors of the world, eating dead animals before they rot. They very rarely kill their own food.

Vultures

Vultures are very clean birds. After eating they will often fly long distances to have a bath.

## A vulture's taste
Vultures don't just eat dead animals. This Egyptian vulture enjoys eggs as well.

The Egyptian vulture loves ostrich eggs but cannot break them with its beak. Instead it uses a stone to crack the egg.

Ostrich egg

## The osprey
Ospreys have such good eyesight that they can spot fish swimming underwater. They swoop down to the surface and seize the fish in their talons, often without landing on the water.

The peregrine falcon—it can dive down toward its prey at 170 mph (270 kph).

69

# Night flyers

As the sun sets, most birds settle down for a good night's sleep. Owls and nightjars, however, are preparing for a night of hunting.

## Owl types
Owls come in lots of sizes and colors and can be found around the world.

**Great horned owl:** this regal-looking owl has ear tufts or "horns."

**Spectacled owl:** this owl lives in the South American rain forest.

**Snowy owl:** this Arctic owl has extra feathers on its feet, to keep it warm, like slippers.

**Burrowing owl:** this owl makes its nest underground.

## Nightjars
Nightjars rest on the ground during the day. At night they hunt, plucking insects out of the air as they fly.

Barn owl

Hooked beaks help to tear up food.

## Hidden from sight
During the day owls sleep, often in branches of trees. Their feathers camouflage them so well, as on these scops owls, that people very rarely notice them.

## Owls
Most owls, such as this barn owl, hunt in darkness and must rely on their amazing eyesight and hearing to help them.

Owls use their sharp talons to catch and grip animals that they eat.

Many owls have velvety fringes around their flight feathers that make their wings very quiet as they fly through the air.

Owl eggs are almost completely round.

What is the smallest owl in the world?

# Hunting by night

All owls eat small animals. They swoop silently on their victims in the dark and grab them in their sharp talons.

In the dark owls sometimes find animals only by the sounds they make.

Tawny owl

Most owl chicks learn to fly when they are two months old. Until then, they are fed by their parents.

Owls eat animals such as mice and small birds.

# Eating

Owls cannot chew so they swallow their food whole. When they have digested the animal, they cough up the bones and fur as a small pellet.

If you tear one of these pellets apart, you can see the whole skeleton of the animal it has just eaten.

An owl's mouth may look quite small but it can open very wide indeed.

Owl pellets

Iranian eagle owl chicks

# Owl chicks

Rather than build nests, owls prefer to lay their eggs in holes of some kind— in trees or buildings. The male and female both help to feed the chicks.

The elf owl — it is only 15 cm (6 in) tall.

71

# Exotic flyers

Tropical rain forests and places with warm climates are filled with exotic and colorful birds, which are often very large.

The toucan uses its massive bill to reach for fruits on the tips of branches.

Although the bill looks heavy, it is hollow and, therefore, very light.

Toucan

This species of toucan lives in the top of the rain forest canopy.

Chestnut-eared aracari

Toucans have two toes facing forward and two facing backward on each foot.

## Toucans
These birds live in the South American rain forest and surrounding areas. They are famous for their huge bills.

## Birds of paradise
These exotic birds are from Papua New Guinea. This raggiana bird of paradise is showing off his beautiful feathers to a female by opening his wings and shaking them at her.

Where do budgerigars live in the wild?

## The parrot family
Parrots are very colorful and often very noisy. They are strong fliers and good climbers. Parrots include macaws, budgerigars, lovebirds, and parakeets.

Rainbow lorikeet

## Crested cockatoos
These parrots, called cockatoos, have a bright yellow crest on their head, which they raise when they are frightened or angry.

Scarlet macaw

## Nuts about nuts
Almost all parrots eat fruit, nuts, and seeds. They are the only birds that hold food up to their mouths using their feet.

Lorikeets are the most colorful of all parrots. They can be found along the east coast of Australia.

Budgerigars are popular as pets for their ability to mimic sounds and "talk."

### Turn and learn
Colorful creatures of the ocean:
pp. 144-151

They live in Australia.

# Game birds

Game birds live most of their lives on the ground. Most are plump with a small head, short wings, and sturdy, strong legs.

Some game birds, like these chickens, are raised specifically to provide food for humans.

Hen

Rooster

## Good-looking males
Like most male game birds, this rooster is more brightly colored than the hen. He uses his fine feathers to attract females.

## Sport
Game birds, such as this male common pheasant, are hunted by humans for sport, which is why they are called game birds.

This male common pheasant has a tough, hooked beak for digging up plant roots and insects to eat.

Males have brightly colored feathers...

The tail drags along the ground behind the male when not spread out.

## Nesting
Most game birds nest in shallow holes in the ground. They can produce more than 20 eggs in one nest—more than most other birds. Females are duller in color than the males, to camouflage them against the ground when nesting.

Some game birds keep their eggs warm not by sitting on them, but by burying them underground.

Where are wild turkeys commonly found?

The peahen chooses a peacock as her mate based entirely on his looks.

Peahen

Peacock

The peacock lifts his tail and shakes it at the female.

## An amazing tail
The male peacock has the most spectacular tail in the animal world. When he wants to attract attention, he raises it high.

## Vertical takeoff
Game birds are strong runners and prefer to run away from danger rather than fly. When very afraid, however, they are capable of rocketing upward quickly with frantic, flapping wing beats.

Reeve's pheasant

When they fly upward at speed, their wings make a whirring sound that can startle enemies.

This male ptarmigan is in its summer plumage.

.. that attract females.

Game bird chicks escape danger on the ground because they are able to run and fly soon after hatching.

### Turn and learn
Courtship displays between birds: pp. 52-53

## Color change
Not all males have bright feathers. Both male and female willow ptarmigans change their colors throughout the seasons so they are always camouflaged.

Pheasant chicks

In the woodlands of the US.

# Globe-trotters

The great advantage birds have is that they can fly. This means they can choose the warmest part of the world to live in at any one time.

## Record holder
The Arctic tern is the biggest traveler of all. Each year, it flies the whole way around the world from the Arctic to the Antarctic and back again.

Arctic tern

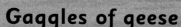

Arctic

EUROPE

ATLANTIC OCEAN

AFRICA

PACIFIC OCEAN

NORTH AMERICA

CENTRAL AMERICA

SOUTH AMERICA

To **Antarctica**

## Migration
Many birds have a summer and a winter home in different places. Their journey from one place to another is called migration.

## Traveling birds
Birds have different travel habits. Some fly nonstop; some rest on the way.

**Song thrush:** these small birds are night fliers and use the stars to find their way.

**Buzzard:** these birds of prey wait for a warm day and glide for long distances.

**Sanderling:** waders eat a lot before leaving so they can fly nonstop.

**Canada goose:** geese are fast fliers, so they use a lot of energy and need to stop frequently to eat.

**Swan:** these birds fly by day or night but rest if visibility gets poor.

**Ruby-throated hummingbird:** this tiny bird flies nonstop across the Gulf of Mexico.

## Gaggles of geese
Each winter, tens of thousands of snow geese leave Canada for a 1,250 miles (2,000 km) trip to California and Mexico. They follow exactly the same route each year.

What proportion of the world's birds migrate each year?

**Turn and learn**

Waterfowl:
**pp. 62-63**
Birds of prey
**pp. 68-69**

## Birds of prey

Hawks, buzzards, and eagles from North America fly south to warmer climates as the winter approaches.

Bald eagle

Eagles use warm air currents to help them glide.

## Knots

Knots leave the Arctic in the fall and fly toward South America. They travel over the 2,000 miles (3,218 km) of ocean nonstop.

## "V" formation

Many birds fly in a "V" formation because the bird in front makes the air easier to fly through for the ones behind.

About one-third of all birds in the world migrate.

# Flightless birds

Some birds cannot fly even though they have wings. Often, as a result of this, they become excellent at running or swimming instead.

## New Zealand birds
There are so few native mammals here that some birds have no need to fly.

**Kakapo:** this flightless bird is the world's rarest parrot.

**Kiwi:** the kiwi lives on the ground. Its feathers are so small they look like fur.

**Takahe:** these birds were almost extinct, but are slowly increasing in numbers.

The ostrich has a long neck and a small head.

## Rapid runners
Ostriches are the fastest bird runners in the world. In fact, they are faster than racehorses—they can reach speeds of 45 mph (75 kph).

Ostrich

The ostrich is the only bird in the world to have just two toes.

## The ostrich
Ostriches are the world's largest birds. They have feathers, which look more like fur, to keep them warm. Even though they can't fly they still have small wings, which are not used for flying, but may have various other uses, like shading their young.

## Moving in flocks
Ostriches and emus live in large groups, called flocks.

Which bird lays the largest eggs?

# Flightless wings

One reason birds have wings is so they can make a quick escape from predators. Birds that don't have predators have no need to fly and may lose this ability over time.

Flightless birds, like this rhea, have wings that they don't use for flying.

## Penguins

A penguin uses its wings as flippers to "fly" underwater. Its wing feathers are short and stiff, which is better for swimming.

## Flightless cormorants

The Galápagos Islands off western South America have no animals that kill birds, so Galápagos cormorants have lost the ability to fly and have very short wings.

## Turn and learn

Penguins:
**pp. 66-67**
Birds' eggs:
**pp. 56-57**

## Rearing rheas

Most birds' eggs are cared for by their mothers, but in the rhea family the father is in charge. He sometimes looks after up to 60 eggs, all from different mothers, in one nest.

Large flightless birds have thick legs, which help them to run fast.

Rheas and emus have three large toes that all face forward.

The father looks after the babies until they are five months old.

The ostrich.

79

# Reptiles and amphibians

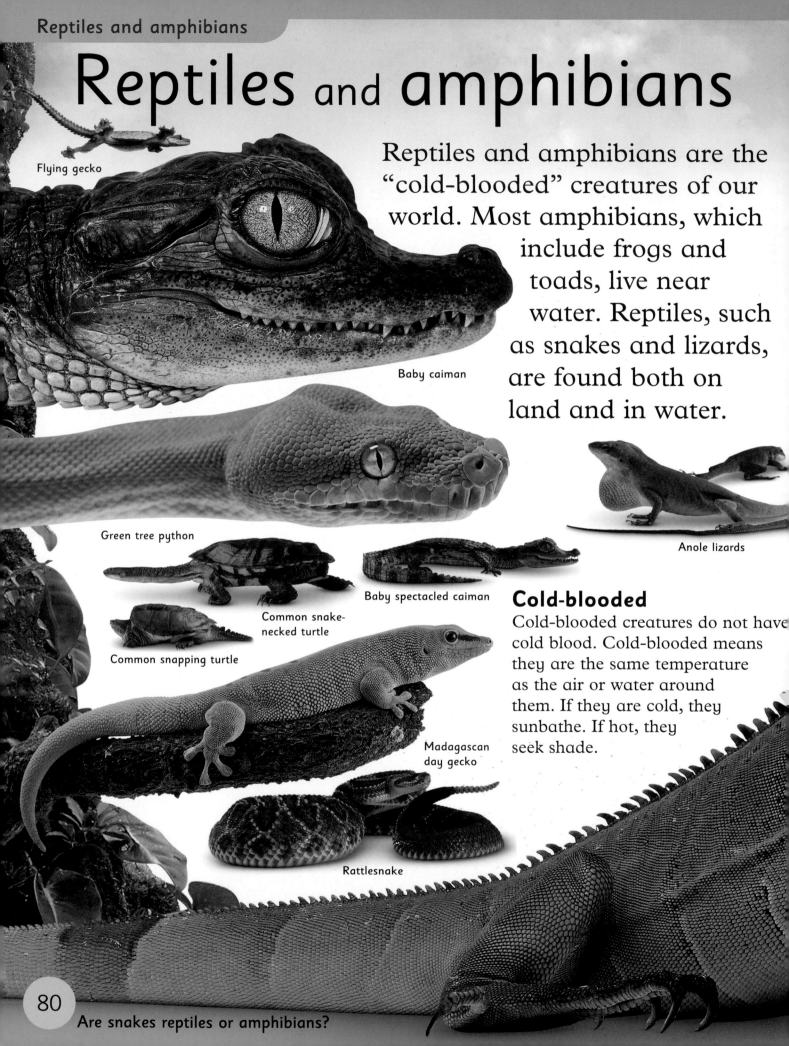

Flying gecko

Reptiles and amphibians are the "cold-blooded" creatures of our world. Most amphibians, which include frogs and toads, live near water. Reptiles, such as snakes and lizards, are found both on land and in water.

Baby caiman

Green tree python

Anole lizards

Common snapping turtle

Common snake-necked turtle

Baby spectacled caiman

## Cold-blooded

Cold-blooded creatures do not have cold blood. Cold-blooded means they are the same temperature as the air or water around them. If they are cold, they sunbathe. If hot, they seek shade.

Madagascan day gecko

Rattlesnake

Are snakes reptiles or amphibians?

Reptiles have scaly skin.

Green anaconda

Wagler's pit viper

Ornate horned toad

Indian starred tortoise

European common frog

Diadem snake

White's tree frog

Asian tree toad

Green iguana

## Picture Detective
Take a look through the reptiles and amphibians pages and see if you can spot who these skins belong to.

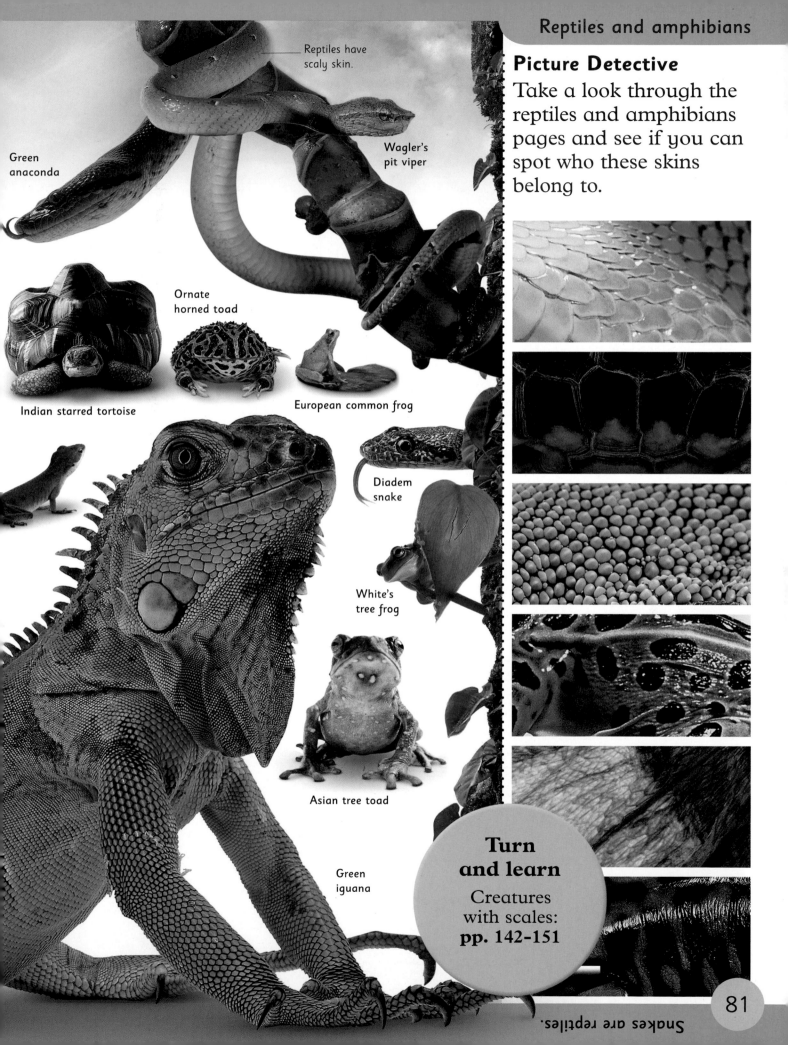

### Turn and learn
Creatures with scales:
pp. 142-151

81

Snakes are reptiles.

# The world of reptiles

Reptiles are mainly egg-laying animals that have a tough skin covered in scales. They live on land and in water.

## The reptile groups
There are four main groups of reptile.

**Turtles and tortoises:** these reptiles all have a shell over their bodies.

**Snakes and lizards:** the majority of reptiles fall into this group.

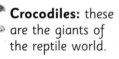

**Crocodiles:** these are the giants of the reptile world.

**Tuataras:** these reptiles are very rare and look a bit like lizards.

## Eating habits
Most reptiles are meat-eaters, except for tortoises, which move too slowly to catch fast-moving prey. Lizards, such as this gecko, can eat half their own weight in insects in one night.

Reptiles can eat huge meals, then go without food for days.

Most reptiles, like this lizard, swing their bodies from side to side when walking.

All reptiles shed their skin from time to time.

Flying gecko

## Hot and cold
Reptiles have scales, which can control how much water they lose through their skin. This means they can live in dry places. They are, however, cold–blooded, and so rely on the climate to keep their bodies warm.

European eyed lizard

## Reptile babies
Nearly all reptiles lay eggs, which hatch into miniature versions of their parents. However, a few, such as this slow worm, give birth to live young.

This lizard, which lives in the desert, basks on rocks to warm its body.

What is the longest snake in the world?

## Living fossils

Tuataras are the only survivors of a reptile group that lived with the dinosaurs millions of years ago. Today, they live on islands off the coast of New Zealand.

Tuataras live in burrows and hunt at night. They can live for 100 years.

## Scaly skin

A reptile's skin is covered with scales made of keratin, like your nails.

**Tortoise:** the shell of a tortoise has lots of large, hard scales on it.

**Lizard:** lizards' scales have stretchy skin between them.

**Crocodile:** these scales are strengthened in between by bony plates.

**Snake:** the skin on snakes has overlapping scales for extra protection.

## Reptile relatives

The reptiles of today are relatives of dinosaurs and look very similar to some of these ancient giants. You can see similarities between the *Tyrannosaurus rex* and this lizard.

*Tyrannosaurus rex*

**Turn and learn**

Snails: pp. 132-133

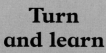

Collared lizard

The reticulated python can reach lengths of 33 ft (10 m).

# Under a shell

You can spot tortoises or turtles because they carry their homes on their backs—these domes, called shells, are attached to their bodies.

Tortoise

## Tortoise or turtle?

The main difference between these two reptiles is that tortoises live on land and turtles live in water.

## Shell shapes

Shells are hard and protect the body. They come in many shapes.

**Starred tortoise:** their high domed shells are difficult to attack.

**African red-necked turtle:** flatter shells help turtles slip through water.

**Red-footed tortoise:** these tortoises have unusually long shells.

Turtles

## Tortoises

Tortoises walk very slowly because of their heavy shells. They have short, stocky legs that support their weight. They spend most of the day eating plants.

## Turtles

Turtles live in water. They sometimes poke their heads out to breathe, but they can also breathe through their skin. Some can stay under the surface for weeks.

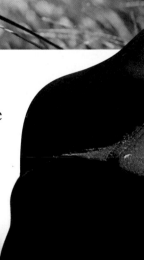

Do tortoises have teeth?

## Eggs and babies

Most turtle and tortoise eggs are completely round, like ping-pong balls. Some are hard, but others are soft to touch. The babies peck their way out of the eggs.

Tortoises and turtles are born complete with their shells.

## Race to the ocean

Turtles return to land to lay eggs—sometimes thousands of them on one beach. When they hatch, the babies all make a rush to the sea, where they will live.

Hinge-back tortoise

## Hiding on the spot

When a tortoise feels threatened, it quickly pulls its legs and head under its shell and keeps very still. The shell is too hard for most animals to eat.

Tortoises' shells are made of bone.

## Galápagos giants

The biggest tortoises in the world live on the Galápagos Islands off the coast of South America. They can be 6 ft (1.8 m) long—that's as long as a man is tall!

The Galápagos tortoise can live to 150 years old.

Experts believe that tortoises lived among the dinosaurs 200 million years ago and have changed very little.

85

No, instead they have sharp jaws that can snip twigs and leaves.

# Introducing lizards

There are over 40,000 different types of lizard, living in habitats ranging from deserts to rain forests. They are particularly fond of hot places.

Most lizards have sharp teeth along the edges of their jaws.

Tokay gecko

## Lizards

Lizards have scaly bodies and four feet that each have five fingers. As lizards grow, they shed their skin about once a month.

Slow worm

## Legless lizards

This slow worm is not a worm—it's a lizard. It looks like a snake but, unlike snakes, it has eyelids and a notched tongue, whereas snake tongues are forked.

Madagascan day gecko

Some lizards have no eyelids. They lick their eyes to clean them.

## Day gecko

Most geckos prefer to be active at night, but this Madagascan day gecko likes the daylight. It lives in forests and eats small insects and fruit.

Which is the fastest lizard on Earth?

## Gliding lizards
Lizards can't fly, but some can glide from tree to tree. This lizard has skin around its body that opens out like a parachute.

## Getting around
Lizards are extremely agile. They can run very fast, and some climb trees—some can even walk on water!

Climbing lizards, such as chameleons, have long claws that can grip branches.

## Eggs
Most lizards lay eggs on the ground.

**Laying:** lizards lay their eggs among leaves on the ground or in sandy holes.

**Eggs:** the eggs are soft and leathery—easy to hatch from.

**Hatching:** after two to three weeks, the lizards hatch.

**Babies:** baby lizards look like their parents.

Chameleon

The chameleon's tail helps it to balance when it perches on thin twigs.

## Sticky fingers
Geckos have special toe pads covered in millions of tiny hairlike spikes. These spikes can grip any surface, so geckos are able climb up walls and even along ceilings.

## Walking on water
When they want to go faster, some lizards, like this crested water dragon, run on their hind legs. The basilisk lizard above can even run for short distances across the surface of the water, its wide feet pushing it along at high speed.

Crested water dragon

The racerunner can run at 18 mph (29 kph)—that's faster than most people can run.

# Hunting and defence

Some lizards are fast runners, so they can get away from danger quickly. They also use their speed to catch smaller animals for food.

The frilled lizard also lashes its tail backwards and forwards.

## Get lost!

When the frilled lizard feels threatened, it doesn't run away. Instead it opens its umbrella-like frill around its neck, rocks its body, and hisses loudly. This is often enough to scare the enemy away.

When the loose skin on a frilled lizard opens out, it looks four times bigger.

### Turn and learn

Insect defence: **pp. 114-115**
Fish defence: **pp. 148-149**

Frilled lizard

What is unusual about a chameleon's eyes?

Chameleon

## Losing the tail

Some lizards are able to detach part of their tail if it is grabbed. Often the tail will carry on wiggling when it has broken off, which can distract the enemy.

This tree skink has broken its tail and is growing a new one.

## Lunch time

Most lizards eat meat. Some eat small animals; some can eat animals bigger than themselves. This chameleon flicks out its enormous, sticky tongue and catches insects on the tip.

The Komodo dragon can grow to 3 m (10 ft) long.

## Enter the dragon

The Komodo dragon is the largest of all lizards. It is so powerful it can catch and kill animals bigger than itself. It has a long forked tongue that it uses to taste the air and search out dead animals. It lives in Indonesia.

Thorny devil

## A touch of venom

The Gila monster is one of only two species of venomous lizards. When it has caught a victim, it chews the venom into its body to kill it.

Gila monster

## Thorny defence

The thorny devil has a very tough defence. Its back is covered with sharp spines, which make picking it up and eating it very difficult indeed.

89

Chameleons can move their eyes in different directions.

# Slithering snakes

Snakes can survive anywhere, from cold climates to the hot deserts and rain forests of the world—you can even find them underwater.

## Getting around

Snakes have no arms and no legs. Instead they have bendy bodies that wriggle over the ground. Some slither forward, others, such as this viper, wriggle sideways.

### Types of snake

Snakes can be divided into four different groups, or families.

**Typical snakes:** this family is the biggest of the four.

**Vipers:** they have long, hinged venomous fangs and live in hot places.

**Constrictors:** kill their prey by squeezing them to death.

**Cobras and kraits:** they are some of the most deadly creatures alive.

A snake's forked tongue flicks in the air to smell food or alert it to enemies.

Red-tailed racer

Snakes have no eyelids, so they cannot blink.

## Snake senses

Snakes can't see or hear very well, but they can smell much better than you or me. They use their forked tongues to smell and taste the air around them.

**Turn and learn**
Snake defense: **pp. 92–93** Snakelike eel: **p. 149**

What is the smallest snake?

Some tree snakes have ridges on their bellies that help them to grip onto branches.

## Tree climbers

Many snakes live in trees, coiling themselves around the branches. They tend to have long tails that they use to climb and balance.

Snakes have very flexible bodies.

Tree snakes find birds' nests in the trees using smell so they can attack and eat the chicks.

## Snakes everywhere

Snake body shapes are adapted to where they live. Ground snakes have heavy bodies to slide through soil, while sea snakes have oarlike tails for swimming.

Most sea snakes, such as this sea krait, are incredibly venomous.

## Hibernating

Snakes can't control their body temperature very well, so those that live in cold climates often have a long sleep, or hibernation, during the winter. They can survive for many months without eating.

Garter snakes

## Laying eggs

Most snakes lay eggs. A mother python coils herself around her eggs to keep them warm, but most snakes leave them and the newly-hatched young to fend for themselves.

The thread snake—it is not much bigger than a worm.

# Attack and defense

All snakes eat animals, including smaller snakes. But other animals also find snakes tasty, so they have to be experts at defending themselves as well as hunting for food.

## Forms of defense

Snakes have many other defenses that protect them from enemies.

**Playing dead:** the grass snake lies with its mouth open pretending to be dead.

**Camouflage:** this viper's coloring camouflages it among the leaves.

**Rattlers:** the rattlesnake shakes its tail to make a loud warning noise.

## Protection

Snakes have various ways of protecting themselves. Some snakes, such as the forest pit viper above, have long fangs containing deadly venom. When threatened, they bite.

When danger threatens, the cobra rears its head and hisses. If this doesn't frighten the enemy away, it strikes.

## Attack

Spitting cobra

Cobras are among the most dangerous snakes on Earth; their venom can easily kill humans. This spitting cobra squirts venom at its victims that can blind them permanently.

92

Which is the most venomous snake in the world?

# Cunning

Snakes creep up on their victims, then lunge at them incredibly quickly. They kill larger victims before they eat them, either by injecting venom or crushing them.

Green cat snake

Many snakes are well camouflaged against their background, which makes it easier for them to stalk victims.

# Eating habits

Snakes eat pretty much anything that moves, from ants and snails to goats and crocodiles. The egg-eating snake can swallow eggs bigger than its head! It then squeezes out the insides and vomits up the shell.

Egg-eating snake

A snake's jaws are elastic so it can swallow huge mouthfuls.

The egg is squashed by muscles inside the snake's body.

# A tight squeeze

Constrictors, such as this anaconda, wrap themselves around their victims and squeeze them until they can't breathe. This snake will eat this large alligator whole!

Snakes can eat so much in one meal that they don't have to feed for weeks.

**Turn and learn**

How lizards defend themselves against enemies: pp. 88-89

93

The fierce snake, found in Australia, is the most venomous.

# Crocodiles and alligators

Lurking beneath the water are the monsters of the reptile world. Meet the wild, ferocious crocodilians.

This animal is a caiman, a type of alligator that lives in Central and South America.

## Fierce crocs

Crocodilians are large, meat-eating reptiles that live in water, but sometimes hunt on land as well. They all have very powerful jaws and teeth.

Crocodilians have three eyelids on each eye—one acts like goggles underwater.

### Crocodilians
There are three types of crocodilian.

**Gharial:** this crocodilian has a long, thin snout.

**Alligator:** it has a shorter, broader snout and lives in the Americas.

**Crocodile:** unlike the alligator, it has teeth showing when its mouth is closed.

*Crocodilians cannot chew.*

## Water beasts
Crocodiles and alligators live in water and are very good swimmers. Their eyes and nostrils are on top of their heads so that they can see, breathe, and hunt with the rest of their bodies underwater.

Spectacled caiman

Most crocodilians live in freshwater rivers and lakes, although a few species also venture out to sea.

## Day to day
Crocodilians lead fairly lazy lives. During the morning and evening they lie on banks basking in the sun with their mouths open. This helps them to warm up or cool down. They spend the night in the water.

How big can crocodiles grow?

## Parenting

Crocodilians make very good parents. Males attract females by bellowing and blowing bubbles. The female lays her eggs near the water and guards them fiercely.

The temperature at which the female keeps the eggs determines whether they are male or female.

Baby crocodile being carried by its mother

Nile crocodile

## Parenthood

The female stays with the eggs until they hatch into tiny versions of their parents. Often the mother will then place the babies into her mouth and carry them to the safety of the water.

They shake and tear meat.

Crocodiles and alligators only eat about 50 meals a year.

**Turn and learn**

Other reptiles that enjoy the water—turtles: **pp. 84-85**

## A large appetite

Crocodilians are some of the world's great meat-eaters. Often, like this crocodile, they wait at the water's edge for an animal to take a drink, then they attack, grabbing it with their massive jaws. They can kill animals bigger than themselves.

Saltwater crocodiles can grow upto a massive 20 ft (6 m)—that's as long as a large car.

95

# The world of amphibians

Amphibians are different from reptiles in that they have smooth skin with no scales. They are born in water, then live on land or in water when they grow up.

Fire
salamander

## Amphibians

There are three main types of amphibian.

**Frogs and toads:** these amphibians have no tails and big back legs.

**Newts and salamanders:** these lizard-shaped animals live on land or in water.

**Caecilians:** these wormlike creatures have no legs.

## Amazing skin

Most adult amphibians, such as this salamander, can breathe through their skin as well as their lungs. For the skin to breathe, it has to be kept moist, which is why most amphibians like to live near water.

## Turn and learn

Mammals that also like to live in water: pp. 44-45

## Colorful creatures

Many amphibians are incredibly colorful creatures. Some are spotted, others are striped, and some are just very bright.

What is the world's most poisonous frog?

# A choice of home

Frogs and toads can live both on land and in water. Some even live in trees.

Land frogs tend to be more rounded in shape than water frogs.

Some frogs live in the tops of tall trees.

## Life in water

Some salamanders spend their whole lives underwater. This cave salamander does not have lungs; it can only breathe through its skin. It is almost completely blind.

## Caecilians

Legless caecilians are rarely seen by humans because they live either underwater or underground. They have pointed heads, which they use like shovels.

If an animal is poisonous it is often a very bright color that warns predators.

## Traveling parents

Each spring, salamanders, newts, frogs, and toads lay their eggs in ponds or streams. Some travel 3 miles (5 km) to get there.

Common newt

97

The most poisonous frog is the golden poison dart frog.

# Frogs and toads

White's tree frog

Frogs and toads have short, tubby bodies and large heads with bulging eyes. They have no visible neck and most have a very wide mouth. Frogs and toads live in lots of different habitats around the world.

Frogs often have longer back legs than toads.

## Frog or toad?

There are not many differences between frogs and toads. Toads tend to have warty skin, while frogs have smooth skin.

*To leap, the frog straightens its legs and pushes away...*

North American leopard frog

Frogs leap to move around and to escape danger.

## Legs and leaping

Frogs are known for their high leaps into the air, which they make using their muscular back legs. Because these are longer than the front ones, they stay folded until it's time to jump!

## Making more frogs

Each spring, thousands of frogs return to the water to find a mate and lay their eggs. Large clumps of these eggs, called spawn, are laid together. They are covered with a jelly that protects them.

Tadpoles live in water until they are frogs.

Spawn

98

Toads' feet are less webbed than frogs'.

Oriental fire-bellied toad

## Time for a chat

Frogs and toads are big talkers. Males croak to attract females and to alarm enemies. This toad has an inflatable vocal sac—a big piece of stretchy skin that helps make an extra-loud sound.

## Running frogs

Not all frogs leap to move around. These African running frogs live in grassy areas where they prefer to remain low, so they raise their bodies off the ground and run.

The African running frog is in the crouching position.

To move, it raises itself up and takes long strides forward.

Webbed feet

## In the water

Frogs and toads are very good swimmers. They have webbed feet, which help them move quickly through the water. They swim by bending their legs in and out, just like people do with the breaststroke.

...from the ground.

Frogs often dive into water for safety.

## Junior frogs

Frog and toad eggs hatch into tadpoles, which are completely different from adults. They look like tiny fish with no legs and long tails. Over four months, the tadpoles gradually grow legs, lose their tails, and turn into mini frogs.

When a frog is fully formed, it can leave the water.

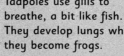

Tadpoles use gills to breathe, a bit like fish. They develop lungs when they become frogs.

Most frogs and toads abandon their eggs, so the tadpoles must look after themselves.

About a quarter of a million!

99

# Hunting and hiding

This four-eyed frog has fake eyes on its rear end to make it look like a big animal.

Frogs and toads eat small animals. But they also make good meals for others because they have no fur, feathers, or claws. They have clever ways to keep from becoming dinner.

## Finding supper
Frog and toad adults are meat-eaters. They have very wide mouths so they can eat fairly big animals.

## Defense
Frogs and toads have many defenses: some use poison, some use camouflage, and others can almost fly!

This toad sits and waits for animals simply to walk past it. It then opens its mouth and swallows them whole.

Ornate horned toad

## Handle with care
Some frogs, like this poison dart frog, are highly poisonous or taste disgusting when eaten. They tend to be very brightly colored—nature's way of warning away enemies.

## A sticky end
Frogs and toads have sticky tongues that grab prey. They shoot out their tongues, grab the insect or small mammal, and swallow it whole! They have to blink when they swallow—their eyeballs help to push the food down their throats.

European common frog

How does the European common toad defend itself?

Tree frogs have huge sticky pads on their feet that help them to grip onto trees.

Flying frogs can change direction in the air.

## Leaping to safety

Some tree frogs are like acrobats. This Wallace's flying frog has webbed feet. When it feels threatened, it leaps into the air, spreads its toes, and uses them as a parachute to glide from branch to branch.

Wallace's flying frog

Asian horned toad

## Spot the toad

The Asian horned toad has one of the best defenses. It simply becomes invisible, using camouflage. Its body is flat, like a leaf, and exactly the same color. Even the flaps over its eyes are leaf-shaped.

### Turn and learn

Defense tactics of insects: pp. 114–115

It stands on tiptoe and blows itself up with air, like a balloon.

# Salamanders and newts

These animals may look like lizards, but they have far more in common with frogs and toads. They have smooth skin and they love the water.

Newts and salamanders have slender bodies and long tails.

Most newts and salamanders live in cool, damp forests.

They must keep their skin damp in order to breathe.

## Newt or salamander?
Newts and salamanders are very similar animals. However, while all newts live on land but breed in water, many salamanders spend their whole lives in the water.

This newt lives under rocks or in caves to keep its skin moist.

How big is the biggest salamander?

## On the move
These creatures normally move slowly but they can move quickly when in danger. They crawl over land and at the bottom of ponds. Newts sometimes swim near the surface of the water.

## Meat to eat
Salamanders and newts are insect- and worm-eaters who like to eat fresh prey. They find their food using smell and sight. Salamanders have long tongues that flick out to catch prey.

This Mandarin salamander is eating an earthworm.

This North American tiger salamander can grow to 15 in (40 cm).

## Colorful displays
Many newts and salamanders are brightly colored. The male sometimes shows off his colors to females when looking for a mate.

## Egg laying
Eggs are laid in the water, and when they hatch, they look very much like frog tadpoles. Unlike frogs, however, they keep their tails when they grow up and gain legs. They live in the water until adulthood.

Great crested newt

These Alpine newts are performing a courtship dance.

## Half-formed
Mexican axolotls are salamanders that have never quite changed fully into adults, but have remained half-formed. They live underwater and are sometimes kept as pets.

# Creepy-crawlies

**Black housefly**

**Lacewing**

**Cave spider**

In this book, creepy-crawlies consist of all the animals that don't belong to the other sections. All creepy-crawlies are invertebrates.

**Spider wasp**

**Common housefly**

**Bush cricket**

**Red giraffe weevil**

**Flea**

**Hornet**

**Tachinid fly**

**Caterpillar**

**Cardinal beetle**

**Dragonfly**

**Locust**

**Giant land snail**

**Spiny-bellied orb weaver spider**

What group do snails belong to?

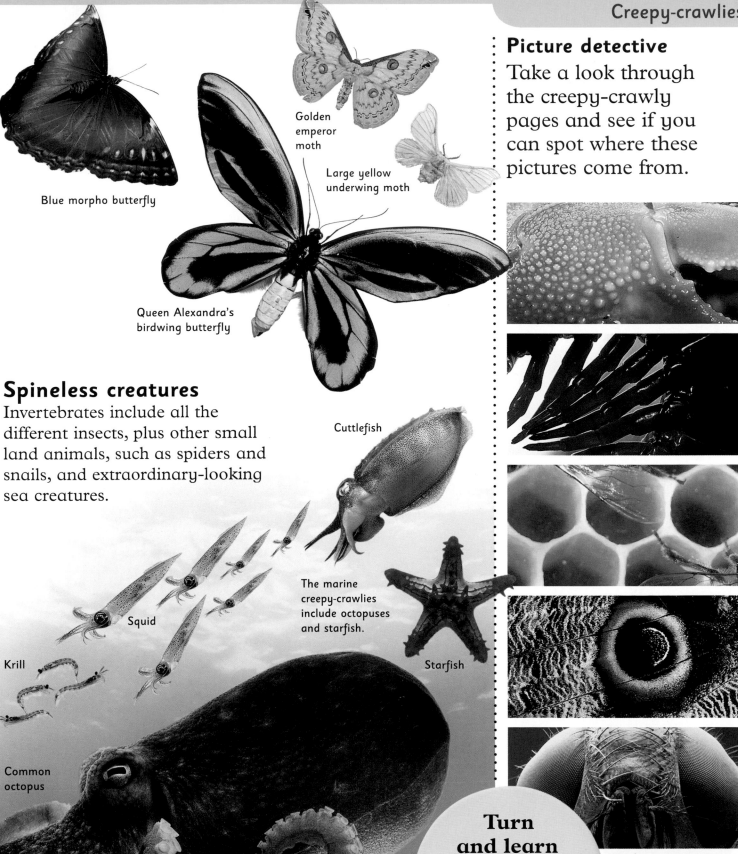

Blue morpho butterfly

Golden emperor moth

Large yellow underwing moth

Queen Alexandra's birdwing butterfly

## Spineless creatures

Invertebrates include all the different insects, plus other small land animals, such as spiders and snails, and extraordinary-looking sea creatures.

Cuttlefish

The marine creepy-crawlies include octopuses and starfish.

Squid

Krill

Starfish

Common octopus

## Picture detective

Take a look through the creepy-crawly pages and see if you can spot where these pictures come from.

## Turn and learn

Sea mammals:
**pp. 44-47**
Sea birds:
**pp. 64-65**

Snails belong to the mollusk group.

# The world of insects

A huge majority of creepy-crawlies are insects. In fact, there are more types of insect in the world than any other animal. They are absolutely everywhere. Some are almost too small to see, while others are surprisingly large.

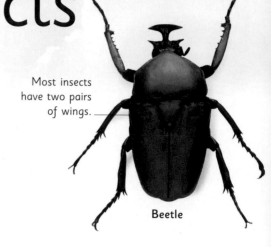

Most insects have two pairs of wings.

Beetle

When a pile of dung appears in Africa, dung beetles are on the scene in minutes.

## What is an insect?

You can tell if a creepy-crawly is an insect because insects always have six legs. They also have three body parts—a head, a thorax, and an abdomen.

## Nature's recycling service

Although many people dislike insects and think of them as pests, they are also essential to our world. In fact, we could not live without them. For instance, dung beetles do a very good job cleaning up dung.

The beetles roll perfect balls of dung in which they lay a single egg. When the egg hatches, the baby eats the dung.

Dung beetle

Aside from honey, what else does a bee produce that we can use?

## Useful insects

Here are some other ways that insects are useful to us.

**Red food dye:** this food coloring is made from the bodies of scale insects.

**Silk:** believe it or not, the silk you wear is made by silk-moth caterpillars!

**Honey:** if there were no bees in the world, we would have no honey.

**Food:** in many cultures around the world, insects such as grubs are a nutritious meal.

## As old as an insect

We know that insects existed 40 million years ago because some were trapped in a tree resin called amber, which hardened and preserved them.

## Pest control

Sometimes insects, such as aphids, destroy huge amounts of farm crops. The best way to get rid of them is to introduce another insect that likes to eat them. Ladybugs are often used for aphid pest control.

Introducing insects that eat other insects is called biological pest control.

Aphid

Ladybug

Aphids breed so quickly that it is difficult to control them.

**Turn and learn**

Beetles: **pp. 120-121**
Bees: **pp. 122-123**

107

Bees produce wax and their venom is used as medicine.

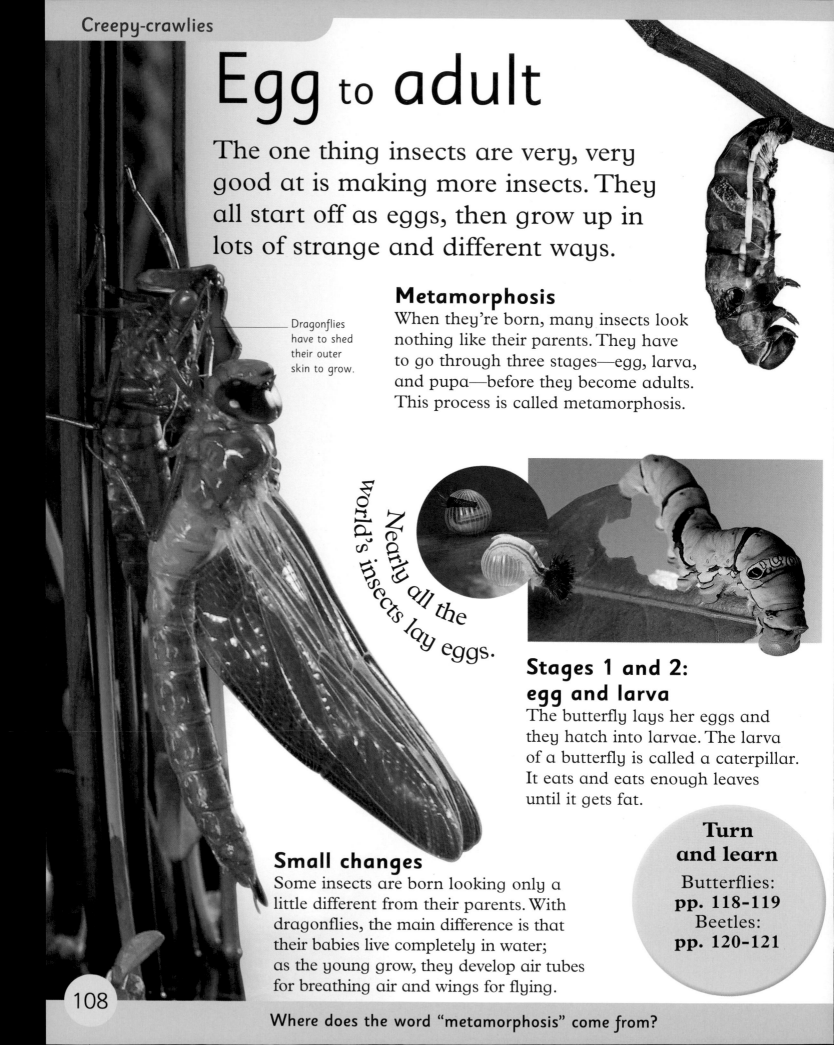

# Egg to adult

The one thing insects are very, very good at is making more insects. They all start off as eggs, then grow up in lots of strange and different ways.

Dragonflies have to shed their outer skin to grow.

## Metamorphosis

When they're born, many insects look nothing like their parents. They have to go through three stages—egg, larva, and pupa—before they become adults. This process is called metamorphosis.

Nearly all the world's insects lay eggs.

## Stages 1 and 2: egg and larva

The butterfly lays her eggs and they hatch into larvae. The larva of a butterfly is called a caterpillar. It eats and eats enough leaves until it gets fat.

## Small changes

Some insects are born looking only a little different from their parents. With dragonflies, the main difference is that their babies live completely in water; as the young grow, they develop air tubes for breathing air and wings for flying.

## Turn and learn

Butterflies:
**pp. 118–119**
Beetles:
**pp. 120–121**

108

Where does the word "metamorphosis" come from?

## Stage 3: pupa

When the caterpillar is big enough, it sheds its skin, fastens itself to a plant stem, and creates a pupa—a hard shell—around itself.

## Stage 4: adult

Inside the pupa an amazing change takes place. Eventually, it splits open and the butterfly emerges.

The caterpillar has to find a safe place to make its pupa.

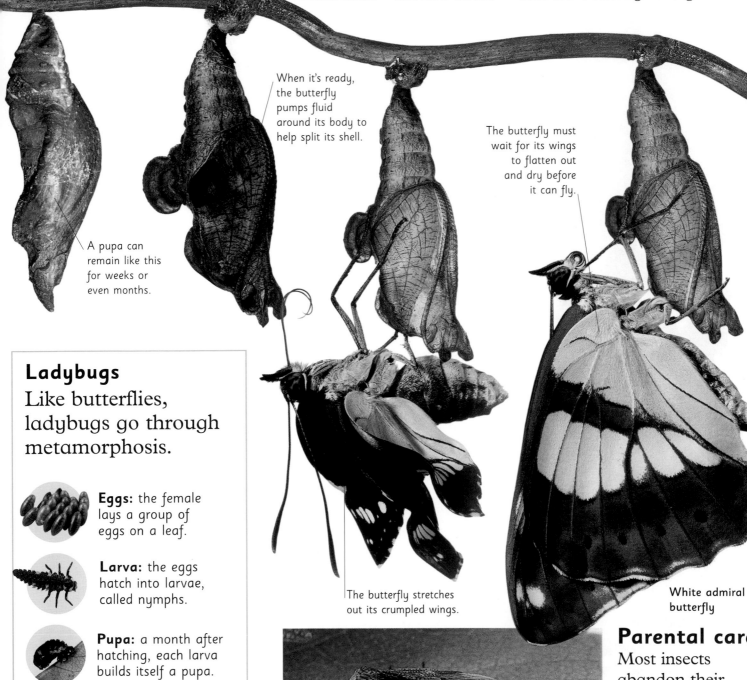

When it's ready, the butterfly pumps fluid around its body to help split its shell.

A pupa can remain like this for weeks or even months.

The butterfly must wait for its wings to flatten out and dry before it can fly.

The butterfly stretches out its crumpled wings.

White admiral butterfly

## Ladybugs

Like butterflies, ladybugs go through metamorphosis.

**Eggs:** the female lays a group of eggs on a leaf.

**Larva:** the eggs hatch into larvae, called nymphs.

**Pupa:** a month after hatching, each larva builds itself a pupa.

**Young ladybug:** A week later, a yellow adult emerges.

**Adult:** After a while, the yellow color turns to red with black spots.

## Parental care

Most insects abandon their eggs after they have laid them. Shield bugs, however, care for and fiercely protect their offspring.

Metamorphosis is Greek for "change of body form."

# On the move

Insects are very good at getting around. Many run, others fly, some jump, and a few even swim!

## Flying

All flying insects have two pairs of wings, but they use them in different ways. Beetles fly with one pair while the second, harder pair folds over the top to protect them.

To fly, the beetle opens out its wing cases, spreads its delicate wings, and jumps into the air.

Cardinal beetle

Wing cases

The flying wings are very fragile, so the beetle needs hard cases to protect them.

### Other wings

Here are some more ways insects use their wings. Many are very good air acrobats.

**Housefly:** flies only use one pair of wings. The other pair look like sticks.

**Dragonfly:** it uses both pairs and can operate each side separately.

**Lacewing:** this insect can use four wings separately and can fly backward.

**Hoverfly:** the hoverfly beats its wings so fast you can barely see them.

This water boatman hangs upside down beneath the surface.

Water boatman

Diving beetle

## Swimming

Some insects spend much of their time under water, using their legs like paddles. Diving beetles have special hairs on their legs that splay out in the water and help them swim.

Caterpillars can crawl up steep twigs.

Which insect can run the fastest?

Darkling beetles can run at 3 ft (1 m) per second.

Locust

Darkling beetle

A tiny flea can jump 100 times its own length. It can also jump 600 times per hour nonstop for three days while looking for an animal to settle on.

## Jumping

Some insects can jump huge distances by using their back legs as powerful springs. If a grasshopper is disturbed, its catapult-like legs help it to get away.

## Running

Insects' legs reflect where they live. Beetles that live under bark have short legs that don't get in the way. Darkling beetles have long legs that let them race across hot sand in the desert.

### Turn and learn

Caterpillars
**pp. 108-109**
Flies:
**pp. 126-127**

Locusts, a kind of grasshopper, can jump upto 3 ft (1 m) high.

These caterpillars have suckers at either end of their bodies to hold onto, and loop up, twigs.

Flea

The green tiger beetle.

# Eating habits

Insects eat a wide range of foods. Some are meat-eaters and some are vegetarians, but most spend their time eating. Insects have mouthparts for either biting and chewing or piercing and sucking.

This hummingbird moth has a long tongue to suck nectar with. It feeds while it is flying.

## Meat-eaters

Many insects eat other insects and have to find cunning ways to catch their meals. This praying mantis hides among leaves and then strikes.

The praying mantis can sit still for a long time waiting for its meal to walk past.

## Vegetarians

Most insects are vegetarians and munch or sip constantly during their lives. Some like to bite and chew food such as leaves; others suck liquid, such as flower nectar, through their tongues.

Antlion larva is sometimes called a "doodlebug."

## Meaty meals

The antlion larva buries itself underground with its open mouth facing the sky and simply waits. When an ant runs over the hole, it falls straight into the antlion's jaws and is eaten swiftly.

How do hawker dragonflies catch insects?

Caterpillars take a long time to digest food.

## Treacherous teeth

Caterpillars are typical vegetarian biters and chewers. They have strong jaws that can get through tough leaves. It is thought that insects eat about 5 percent of all leaves in the world.

### Turn and learn

Butterflies and moths:
pp. 118-119

A butterfly lays her eggs on a leaf that will be the caterpillar's first meal—it doesn't have to travel very far to find food.

This weevil has drilled a hole in an acorn.

## Alligator tears

A butterfly has a long tongue called a proboscis, which it uses to sip liquids. The flambeau butterfly has very strange taste in food; it likes to sip alligators' tears. What a brave insect!

They grab them out of the air.

## Acorn eater

The acorn weevil only likes to eat acorns. It pierces the nut with its snout, chomps the insides using jaws at the snout's end, and finally sucks up the chewed food.

# Defense

Many insects make delicious meals for other animals. So it is very important that they have some defense against their enemies.

Orchid mantis

## Camouflage
A good way for insects to "disappear" is to hide among plants. This white orchid mantis is hiding in plants that are the same color that it is. Can you find it?

The orchid mantis can change color from pink to white, depending on what color flower it is on.

**Turn and learn**
How fish defend themselves: pp. 148-149

## Lost among leaves
This katydid, a kind of bush cricket, looks so much like a leaf that it even has veins on its back. All it has to do is keep very still.

The butterfly's "eye"

Which insects look exactly like brown twigs?

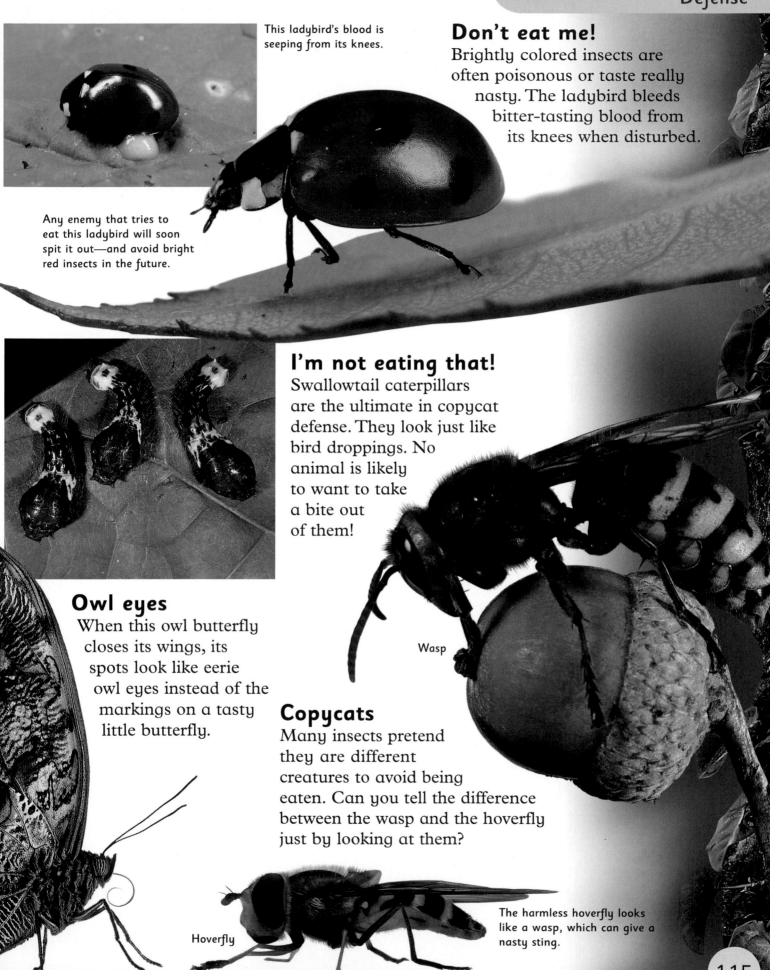

This ladybird's blood is seeping from its knees.

## Don't eat me!
Brightly colored insects are often poisonous or taste really nasty. The ladybird bleeds bitter-tasting blood from its knees when disturbed.

Any enemy that tries to eat this ladybird will soon spit it out—and avoid bright red insects in the future.

## I'm not eating that!
Swallowtail caterpillars are the ultimate in copycat defense. They look just like bird droppings. No animal is likely to want to take a bite out of them!

Wasp

## Owl eyes
When this owl butterfly closes its wings, its spots look like eerie owl eyes instead of the markings on a tasty little butterfly.

## Copycats
Many insects pretend they are different creatures to avoid being eaten. Can you tell the difference between the wasp and the hoverfly just by looking at them?

Hoverfly

The harmless hoverfly looks like a wasp, which can give a nasty sting.

Stick insects look exactly like small twigs.

# Pests and plagues

Insects are small, but they can do a huge amount of damage. It may be hard to believe, but these are some of the most dangerous creatures alive.

Cockroaches have tough bodies and are very difficult to kill.

## Unwanted guests
Once cockroaches move into your home they are very difficult to get rid of. They eat rotten food and spread diseases around the house. They also make a house smell.

## Some more pests
Humans have a hard time controlling pests. For thousands of years, we have been trying to find ways to get rid of them.

**Colorado beetle:** this little beetle can destroy entire potato fields.

**Common clothes moth:** these moths love to eat wool clothes.

**Long-horned beetle:** these beetles can destroy entire forests.

Cockroach

## Turn and learn
Tiny animals that live on your body and can make you sick:
**pp. 140–141**

## Head lice
The head louse is a tiny insect that grips onto your hair so tightly that it is tricky to remove. It drinks blood from your head and makes your scalp itchy. Its eggs are called nits.

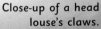
Close-up of a head louse's claws.

What are bedbugs?

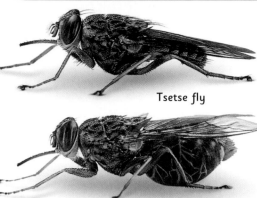

Tsetse fly

## Bloodsuckers

The tsetse fly is a bloodsucker. It pierces the skin of humans and other animals and sucks their blood. Here you can see the fly with an empty and a full belly. It spreads a disease called sleeping sickness.

## Hungry locusts

When the rains fall in Africa, millions of locusts sometimes gather together and move in huge groups, or swarms. They eat everything in sight, and there are so many of them that they blot out the sunlight.

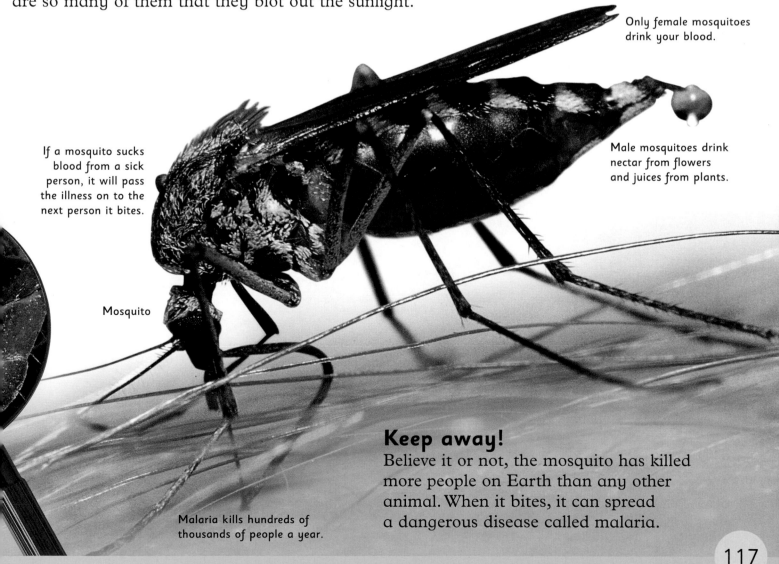

Only female mosquitoes drink your blood.

If a mosquito sucks blood from a sick person, it will pass the illness on to the next person it bites.

Male mosquitoes drink nectar from flowers and juices from plants.

Mosquito

## Keep away!

Believe it or not, the mosquito has killed more people on Earth than any other animal. When it bites, it can spread a dangerous disease called malaria.

Malaria kills hundreds of thousands of people a year.

Bedbugs are tiny insects that suck your blood when you sleep.

# Butterflies and moths

Brown brindled beauty moth

Butterflies and moths are unique insects because their wings are covered in tiny scales. They look alike, but there are a few slight differences.

Hartig's brahmaea moth

Arctiid moth

There are no silk moths left in the wild—they are all bred to make silk.

Silk moth

## Which is which?
Butterflies have club-shaped antennae, or feelers, and moths tend to have feathery or plain antennae. Butterflies are also generally more colorful than moths.

Purple emperor butterfly

The moon moth has no mouth. It only lives long enough to lay eggs and doesn't have time to eat before it dies.

Red glider butterfly

Monarch butterfly

Madagascan moon moth

## Resting
Butterflies come out by day and moths emerge at night. When moths rest, they open their wings, while butterflies rest with their wings closed.

Eighty-eight butterfly

Banana eater butterfly

## Scaly wings
Both butterflies and moths have tiny scales on their bodies and wings that overlap like tiles on a roof.

This Millar's tiger moth has its wings open.

This peacock butterfly has its wings closed.

What is the biggest butterfly in the world?

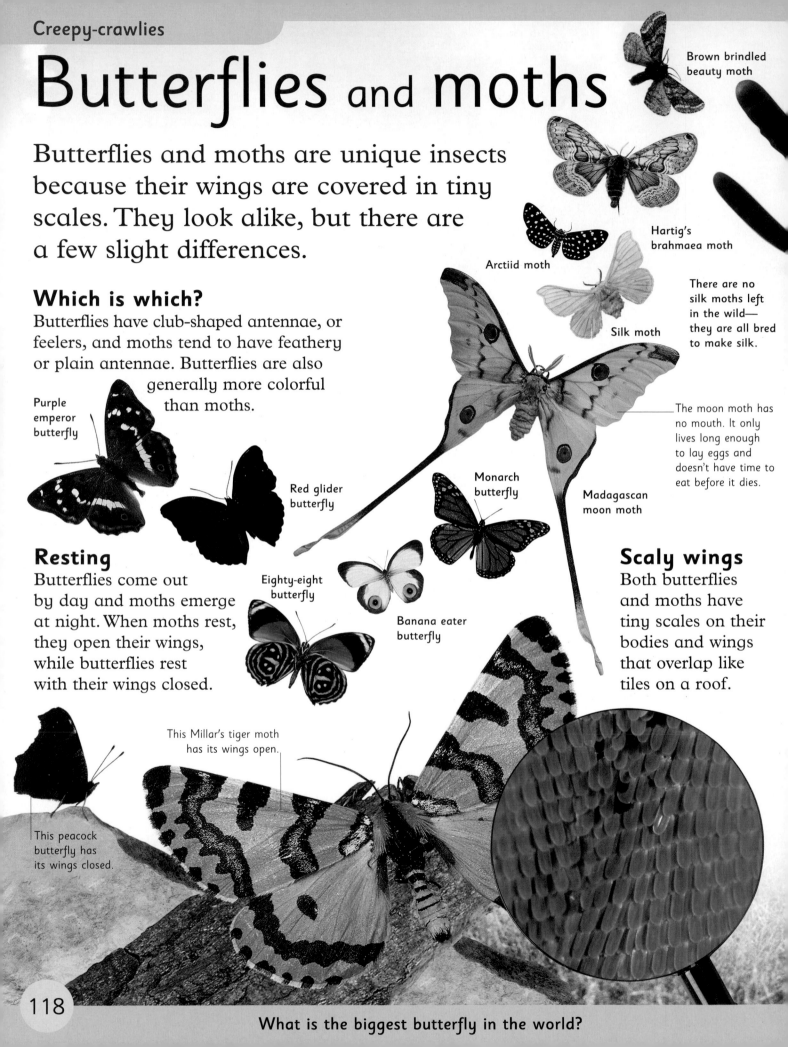

## Incredible migration

Monarchs are unusual butterflies. When the cold weather sets in, they undertake an incredible journey. They travel from Canada to the warm weather in California and Mexico. They can cover 80 miles (130 km) in a day.

Trees are often covered in monarch butterflies as they rest.

Antennae are used for smelling.

Caterpillars spend most of their time eating.

## Tasty tidbits

Caterpillars can make tasty snacks for some animals, so they have cunning ways of fooling their enemies.

**Puss moth caterpillar:** it rears its colorful head when threatened.

**Elephant hawk-moth caterpillar:** it can change the shape of its body to look like a snake.

**Postman caterpillar:** it is covered in long spines.

A butterfly keeps its tongue rolled into a coil until it wants to eat. It then unrolls it and uses it like a straw.

## Eating

Butterflies and moths hatch as caterpillars, which eat in a completely different way from the adults.

## Hungry caterpillar

Caterpillars have strong jaws, which they use to chew leaves. When they become butterflies, their mouthparts change—a butterfly has a long tongue, called a proboscis, which it uses to sip liquid.

Tongue, or proboscis

### Turn and learn

How caterpillars change into butterflies: pp. 108-109

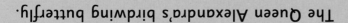

# Beetles and bugs

These amazing creatures are found all over the world, from mountaintops to scorching deserts.

## Beetles
Beetles are the most heavily armored of all insects. They have biting and chewing mouthparts.

The African Goliath beetle is the biggest beetle in the world.

The diving beetle uses its legs as paddles.

## Diving beetles
Most beetles live on land, but the diving beetle catches its food—tadpoles and even small fish—in the water. In order to breathe, it tucks a bubble of air under its wings before every dive.

## Beetles
Beetles are often bright and colorful.

**Scarab:** this beautiful golden scarab is found in South America.

**Chafer beetle:** these lovely beetles vary hugely in size and color.

**Weevil:** this bright blue weevil is found in Papua New Guinea.

**Frog beetle:** frog beetles have colorful bodies with a metallic, shiny look.

How do most bugs taste their food?

## Glow in the dark

Glowworms are not worms—they are beetles. They have a special organ in their bodies that lights up in the dark. They flash their bodies at night to communicate with each other.

Glowworms can sometimes be seen at night glowing and flashing in their thousands.

Glowworms are found all over the world.

## Bugs

Members of the bug family look a lot like beetles, but they have a feeding tube that pierces and sucks up their food. They cannot bite and chew.

## Bugs

They are small, but some can be very aggressive!

 **Shield bug:** it is known as the "stink bug" because it can let out a foul smell.

 **Coreid bug:** this bug waves the flaps on its legs to scare predators.

 **Aphid:** this little creature is a pest. It attacks garden plants.

 **Assassin bug:** it kills other insects and sucks out their insides.

## Clicking cicadas

Cicadas, a type of bug, are the noisiest of insects. They can be heard up to 1 mile (1.5 km) away. They make noise by vibrating drumlike pads the sides of their bodies.

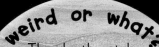

**weird or what?**

The deathwatch beetle eats through wood. When it wants to attract another beetle's attention, it bangs its head against the wood. Sometimes people hear the tapping in their houses.

Some cicada species can live for 17 years!

Most bugs taste their food through their feet.

# Bees and wasps

You may think bees and wasps simply buzz a lot and sting, but they are actually some of the most intelligent insects around.

## Bees
Bumblebees and honeybees live in large colonies, working together as a group. Worker bees spend much of their lives gathering nectar from plants, which they turn into honey.

Bumblebees do not produce large amounts of honey.

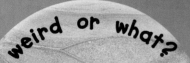

When a honeybee knows that a flower is full of nectar, it does a special waggling dance to show other worker bees where to go to collect it.

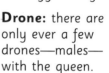
The bee has special baskets on its legs for collecting pollen.

Worker bees cannot lay eggs. Only the queen provides new offspring.

Honey is their food.

## Comb
A honeybee's home is a miniature city made of wax, produced by the bees, in cell shapes. This is called a honeycomb. Some cells hold a baby larva and some hold honey.

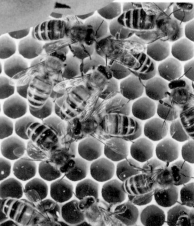

122

True or false: honeybees die immediately after they sting.

## Nests

Wasps either live alone (solitary wasps) or in large groups (social wasps). Those that live together build large nests made out of dead wood that they chew into paper.

The queen begins building the nest until her first babies are big enough, after which they take over.

The wasps chew and chew dead wood until it becomes pulpy. It then dries into paper.

Bees and wasps have powerful biting mouthparts.

Common wasp

## Wasps

There are many different families of wasp. Most adults have a narrow waist between their second and third segments and large eyes.

## Stings

Wasps and bees have yellow and black stripes that warn people they are venomous. They only sting when they feel threatened or they are defending their home.

Sting

## Living alone

Many wasps do not live in groups, but prefer to live alone. They are called solitary wasps. They are mostly parasitic, laying their eggs on other insects.

Ichneumon wasp (solitary)

## Moving in swarms

When a new queen is born, she will leave with a group of wasps to build and rule her own nest. The wasps all fly off together in a group called a swarm. In this picture they are resting.

True, they can only sting once.

# Ants and termites

There are more termites and ants on Earth than any other type of insect—there are trillions of them! They live in groups called colonies.

Ant

## Termites

Most termites live in tropical areas. Each colony has a queen, who is the chief, and she has a king. Workers clean and feed, and soldiers guard.

## Ants

There are many different types of ant, one or more living in almost every part of the world. These are leaf-cutter ants; they collect leaves and turn them into food.

In some species, the queen grows into a huge egg-laying machine, producing 30,000 eggs in a day!

Termite soldiers

The fierce termite soldiers have big jaws to bite anything that disturbs their queen or their home.

## Termite mounds

Some termites live in huge mounds, which they build using soil, saliva, and their droppings—one piece on top of another, like bricks. Some mounds can be up to 25 ft (7 m) high.

The walls of termite mounds are so hard that you would need an ax to get into them!

## Inside the mound

Each termite mound contains a huge network of rooms and passages. The queen and her eggs stay in the nursery, which is located in the center.

Which ants live in colonies of up to 300,000 individuals?

## Working together

Some ants and aphids—a type of bug—are very good at keeping each other happy. The aphids give off a sweet liquid that the ants like to sip, so in return the ants guard the aphids and protect their eggs for them.

Ants and aphids often live on trees together.

**Turn and learn**

Aphids and other bugs: pp. 120-121

There are 12,000 different kinds of ant in the world.

## Pantry pals

Honeypot ants live in the desert. The workers fill chosen ants with nectar, which they turn to honey and store in their big bellies. When food is scarce they vomit it up and feed the colony with it. The honeypots are too big to move.

Wood ants live in these enormous colonies.

# Flies

There is no escaping them—flies are all over the place. Lots of people hate them because many spread diseases and a lot of them bite. But flies have their uses, and we couldn't live without them.

## Disease carriers

Flies like rotting food and their sticky feet can carry bacteria from one piece of food to another, which can spread nasty diseases.

Housefly

A fly vomits on food to turn it to liquid, and then sucks it up.

A fly uses special mouthparts to suck up food.

## Fly babies

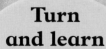

Flies often lay their eggs, which hatch into maggots, in manure or garbage. Unlike adults, maggots do not have wings, and they chew rotten food rather than suck it up. They eventually turn into pupas, then flies, just like caterpillars turn into butterflies or moths.

Maggots

## Flight

Flies are very good fliers, which is why they are difficult to swat. This hoverfly can beat its wings up to 1,000 times per second! Sometimes it changes direction so quickly that it seems to disappear.

### Turn and learn

Other pests:
**pp. 116–117**
Metamorphosis
**pp. 108–109**

Where do mosquitoes lay their eggs?

## Sticky feet

The housefly has sticky feet, which enable it to walk up walls and across ceilings. It rubs its feet together to clean off dust and dirt, keeping them sticky.

## A fly's uses

If there were no flies in the world, there would be a lot more rotting food and dead animals around. Although we may think flies are nasty, they actually do a very good job of eating trash.

## Fly collection

There are many species of fly, and they come in all shapes and colors.

**Tachinid fly:** these flies are small, bristly, and often brilliantly colored.

**Crane fly:** this fly looks a like a big mosquito but doesn't bite.

**Robber fly:** this fly has extraordinary, feathery back legs.

**Bee fly:** these little flies look like bees and are stout and very hairy.

A fly has compund eyes, which means it sees the world in the form of thousands of tiny images that merge into one big picture.

Bluebottle fly

Flies have fine hairs on their legs that can sense tiny movements.

Mosquitoes lay their eggs in still water, which is why they often live near ponds.

127

# Other creepy-crawlies

There are many creepy-crawlies scuttling around our planet that are not insects. Some live on land, others live in freshwater or in the sea. They come in all kinds of weird and wonderful shapes.

## The worm family

Segmented worms, such as earthworms, are simple animals that have a head at one end, a tail at the other, and lots of segmented body parts in between. They live on land or in water.

## Arachnids

Spiders, scorpions, ticks, and mites belong to a land-dwelling family called arachnids. All arachnids have eight legs and two body parts.

Tarantula

Despite their reputation, most spiders are harmless to humans.

A tarantula has hairs on its legs that can cause irritation to humans. When the spider is annoyed, it flicks them out at the enemy.

**Turn and learn**

Spiders and scorpions: pp. 130-131

How big can spiders grow?

## Odd sea creatures

The sea contains some very strange animals. Here are a few:

 **Sponge:** these animals were once thought to be plants.

**Starfish:** most starfish have five arms, which they use to crawl.

 **Anemone:** these flowerlike sea animals have no brains.

Snail

Snails are found on land and in the sea.

## Mollusks

Slugs, snails, squid, and oysters are mollusks. Some live on land and some live in water.

The octopus, which is also a mollusk, is a very intelligent creature.

Centipede

Millipede

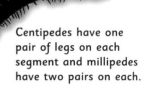

Centipedes have one pair of legs on each segment and millipedes have two pairs on each.

## Centipedes and millipedes

If you try to count the legs on an insect and you find there are too many, chances are you have found a centipede or millipede. They have lots and lots of legs.

## Crustaceans

Most crustaceans, such as lobsters, crabs, and shrimp, live in water. Only wood lice live on land. They have hard-shelled bodies and eyes on stalks..

Lobster

Some spiders can grow as big as dinner plates!

# Spiders and scorpions

Spiders and scorpions are the best-known members of the arachnid family. They are two of the most feared creatures on Earth, despite the fact that most do not attack humans.

## Spiders

There are about 40,000 species of spider in the world. They can all bite, but most are not dangerous to humans.

Of all spiders, jumpers have the best eyesight.

Jumping spider

This is the silk line that the jumping spider attaches to something before it jumps.

The jumping spider spots a fly and leaps, attached to a line of silk,

Ticks are so small that you can barely see them.

## Scorpions

Scorpions live in warm climates and feed on insects. A scorpion holds its prey with its big pincers and paralyzes it with the sting on the end of its tail, which it bends right over its back.

## Bloodsucking ticks

A tick is also an arachnid. When it feeds, it attaches itself to an animal and bites its flesh. When it has drunk enough blood, it drops off.

This jungle scorpion is carrying her babies on her back until they can look after themselves.

Sting

Scorpion

Some scorpions grow to lengths of 6 in (15 cm).

How many eyes do spiders have?

## Webs

All spiders produce silk from inside their abdomens. Most weave nests or webs with it, while jumping spiders use it to anchor themselves to one object while they leap to another.

Spiders build their webs and wait patiently for insects to fly into them. They then wrap the insects in jackets of silk and eat them.

Water spiders even make underwater webs that keep an air bubble in place.

## Water spiders

Most spiders live on land, but some, such as the water spider, live underwater. To breathe, a water spider traps air in a bubble, which it anchors to a plant.

Most spiders remain with their eggs, looking after them until they have hatched.

so quickly that the fly doesn't have a chance to escape.

Egg sac

## Eggs and babies

Spider's silk is also used to build nests or to attach eggs to the spider to carry around. This spider, however, holds the eggs in her jaws until they hatch.

### Turn and learn

Bloodsuckers: **pp. 116-117**
Vampire bats: **pp. 30-31**

Most spiders have eight eyes!

# Strange land creatures

There are lots of interesting creepy-crawlies living in the undergrowth. Some are large, others small, some have lots of legs, and some no legs at all.

## Snails

One of the slowest movers on land is the snail. When it feels threatened it doesn't have to rely on speed; it simply pulls itself inside its shell.

The shell of the snail is attached to its back.

Snail

A garden snail's shell always coils in a clockwise direction.

Giant tiger centipede

## Centipedes

The word centipede means "100 feet," but centipedes actually have a lot fewer. Giant tiger centipedes are found in jungles. They eat spiders and insects, which they kill with venom.

How big is the biggest snail in the world?

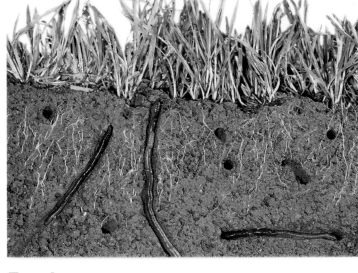

When pill wood lice are frightened, they curl up into tight balls.

# Wood lice

Wood lice look like insects, but they are related to crabs and lobsters. They live in dark, damp places to keep from drying up, and they eat rotten leaves and wood.

# Earthworms

Earthworms are long, thin creatures that live underground. They push their way through the soil, eating rotting plants and animals.

Slugs and snails have one muscly foot that they use to slither around on.

Some millipedes roll into balls if they sense danger.

Slug

# Millipedes

Millipedes have lots of legs—sometimes as many as 300! But this doesn't mean they run fast. They have to move their legs in waves to stop them from hitting one another.

# Slimy slugs

Slugs are similar to snails but they have no shell. They move by sliding over slime that they squeeze out through their foot. Sometimes they leave a shiny trail behind them.

Slugs spend the day hiding and feed at night.

A leech is a type of worm that sucks blood from animals.

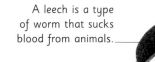

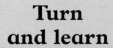

**Turn and learn**

Sea slugs and sea snails: pp. 136-137

The Giant African snail can grow to the size of your forearm.

# Sea crustaceans

It's easy to see how these creatures got their name—they are covered in hard plates that act like a crust. Most crustaceans live in water.

## Crusty creatures

A lobster has a hard skeleton on the outside of its body like other crustaceans, two eyes on stalks, and a pair of long antennae. Most lobsters live among rocks on the seafloor.

## Crabs

Crabs are armed with a pair of pincers that they use to nip their enemies very hard when they feel threatened. Crabs live on the seashore and the seabed.

The crab's eyes are at the ends of these stalks.

Crabs use their pincers to crack the shells of other animals and to pick up food.

Fiddler crab

Which crustacean lives permanently on land?

## Barnacles

On many seashores, millions of barnacles cling to rocks. They start life as tiny larvae; when they settle on a rock they fasten themselves to it, grow a hard case around themselves, and stay there for life.

## Cleaning up

Some shrimp get their food in a very unusual way—by cleaning the mouths and scales of willing fish. They use their delicate pincers to pick out dead skin and tiny creatures.

## Red crab alert!

Christmas Island in the Indian Ocean has a community of about 100 million red crabs. Each year at the same time, every single crab crosses the island to lay its eggs on the beach. What a traffic jam!

The crabs start walking when the rains come to the island.

## Finding a home

Hermit crabs have softer bodies than other crabs, so to protect themselves they hunt for empty shells to live in. Often the crabs fight for a good shell.

Goose barnacles

These barnacles are attached to rocks by long stalks.

Hermit crabs

**Turn and learn**

Land crustaceans: **p. 133**

You are more likely to see wood lice in the yard than on the seashore.

# Sea mollusks

Sea mollusks come in many weird and wonderful shapes. Who would have thought that octopuses and scallops are related? Some live on land, others live in water.

Octopus

**Clever creatures**
Octopuses and squid have large brains and are very intelligent. All octopuses and squid have eight arms.

## Meet the family
Squid and cuttlefish are the nearest relatives to octopuses.

**Blue-ringed octopus:** this octopus can change color and has a deadly venom.

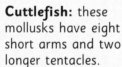
**Cuttlefish:** these mollusks have eight short arms and two longer tentacles.

**Squid:** squid are torpedo shaped and can swim very fast.

This octopus has a crab in its jaws.

The ink can also numb the enemy, stopping it from chasing the octopus or squid farther.

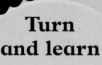

**Turn and learn**
Reptiles with shells: **pp. 84–85**
Land slugs: **pp. 132–133**

## Ink squirting
When octopuses and squid feel threatened by another sea creature, they squirt ink out of their bodies to confuse it and create a smoke screen.

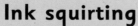
Do octopuses have teeth?

## Sea snails

Conches, whelks, and winkles are all sea snails. They have shells and can commonly be seen clinging to rocks. Most eat plants, but some eat other small sea creatures.

Whelk

## Sea slugs

Strangely enough, some slugs live in water. Like their cousins, they have no shells for protection. Some are poisonous, while others, such as this lettuce slug, camouflage themselves from predators.

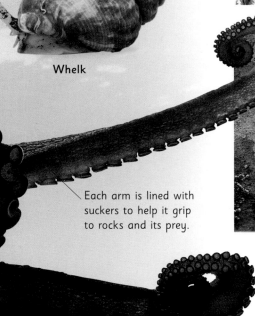

Each arm is lined with suckers to help it grip to rocks and its prey.

## Limpets

Limpets have cone-shaped shells that protect them. They cling to rocks and graze on algae, a type of plant, wandering around using their muscular foot.

Limpets have been grazing on this rock—you can see the trails they have made.

Limpets can often be seen in clusters on rocks.

Limpet

## Two-hinged shells

Oysters, mussels, scallops, and clams all have a shell that is hinged into two parts that can open and close. They open them to suck food in and breathe, and keep them tightly shut to protect themselves.

Giant clam

## Quick scallop

Queen scallops can move surprisingly quickly through the water. They clap the two parts of their shell together and this movement propels them backward.

The black dots around the shell are eyes.

Queen scallop

137

No, but they have sharp beaks.

# Brainless wonders

There are a lot of very strange sea creatures. Some don't even look like animals at all. The one thing all the animals on these pages have in common is that they have no brains.

Some sponges can grow so big that divers can swim inside them.

## The coral reef
Believe it or not, coral is an animal, or rather, lots of tiny animals—called polyps—stuck together. They create hard outer skeletons that form their home and give coral its hard ridges.

## Sponges
Sponges look like plants but are actually animals, even though they are attached to the seabed. The bright colors often make the seafloor look like an underwater garden.

## Sea urchin
This spiked creature may look harmless, but you wouldn't want to step on one. Sea urchins are covered in sharp spines that protect their soft bodies.

Sea urchins

Sea urchins have tube-shaped feet and can walk across the seafloor.

**Turn and learn**
Venomous sea creatures: pp. 148–149

Which is the most venomous creature in the sea?

## Starfish

Most starfish have five arms that stick out from their center. They have some strange-looking relatives too.

**Starfish:** almost all starfish look like this one, with five arms.

**Sunstar starfish:** this starfish is unusual—it has 12 arms.

**Gray starfish:** this starfish has red nodules all over it.

**Brittlestar:** it has longer arms than a starfish and moves more easily.

**Sea cucumber:** this starfish cousin has 8 to 30 feet around its mouth.

## Jellyfish

A jellyfish is an unusual creature—it has no brain, no bones, and no heart! It moves through the water like a big umbrella, opening and closing to move along.

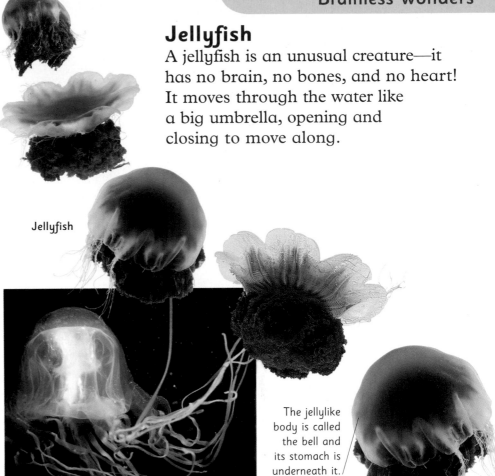

Jellyfish

The tentacles of the box jellyfish act like fishing lines to catch food.

The jellylike body is called the bell and its stomach is underneath it.

## Sea anemones

Sea anemones look like pretty sea flowers, but they can give lethal stings to small animals. They use their venomous tentacles to stun fish before they eat them.

This starfish is eating a mussel.

The starfish pushes its stomach through its mouth and into the shell to eat it.

Dahlia anemones

## Eating habits

The mouth of a starfish is underneath its body. It uses its arms to crack open mussel shells, then gobbles up the creature inside.

139

The box jellyfish is the most venomous thing in the sea.

# The world of microlife

Some creepy-crawlies, whether insects or other tiny creatures, are so small that you can't see them unless you look through a microscope. They are everywhere, however—even in your eyelashes!

Some plankton are as big as your fingernail; others are too small to see.

## Unwelcome guests

Tiny animals like to share our bodies with us. Some are helpful guests, but others we would rather get rid of, like this head louse.

Head louse

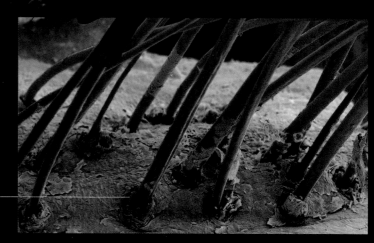

Eyelash mite

## Eyelash mites

Like everyone else in the world, you have had tiny mites living on your eyelashes since you were a baby. They are harmless, but they can make your eyes itch a little.

**Turn and learn**
Pests and plagues: pp. 116–117

Head lice make your scalp itch.

Some of these tiny bacteria give you an upset stomach.

How many dust mites could you fit in one bed?

A lot of plankton, like this larva, are the babies of many kinds of sea creatures.

## Sea microlife

The oceans are full of plankton, a group of different microscopic creatures. There are so many of them that the sea is like a big, thick plankton soup. Many fish eat plankton, but there are always plenty more.

Plankton

Some huge whales eat only tiny plankton.

## Bacteria

There are about 300 types of bacteria that live on your teeth! They are not animals, but they are some of the smallest living things on Earth. This is the tip of a needle (magnified many times) and the tiny orange specks are bacteria. Some of them can make you sick, but most are friendly.

## House dust mites

These ferocious-looking creatures are so small that you can't see them. But they are all around you. Dust mites live in your home and love to eat the dead, flaky skin that you shed around the house. Some people are allergic to them.

House dust mite

Your bed already has about 1 million of them in it!

141

# Fish

Fish truly dominate the waters of the world. They come in many shapes and sizes, from huge whale sharks to strange seahorses and fish so tiny you can barely see them.

Zebrafish

Yellow tang

Long-nosed gar

Cuban hogfish

Royal gramma

Zebra pipefish

Golden-eyed dwarf cichlids

Emperor angelfish

Sticklebacks

Thornback ray

Three-striped dwarf cichlids

Clown triggerfish

Boxfish

How many different species of fish can be found on Earth?

**Copperband butterfly fish**

**Yellow wrasse**

## Picture detective

Take a look through the fish section and see if you can spot the owners of these colorful skins.

**John Dory**

**Ram cichlid**

**Goldfish**

**Seahorse**

## Bony fish

Most fish are bony, which means they have a hard skeleton inside them. Sharks are not bony fish, but have a skeleton made of cartilage—a material that is softer than bone.

### Turn and learn
Seahorse:
**p. 151**
Sharks:
**pp. 152-153**

There are about 32,800 species of fish in seas, rivers, and lakes.

# The world of fish

Fish have been around for 400 million years! They live in oceans, rivers, and lakes. Wherever you find water, you can bet there are plenty of fish swimming around.

## Types of fish
There are over 30,000 types of fish, which fall into three groups.

**Bony fish:** 95 percent fish in the world are bony fish with hard skeletons.

**Cartilaginous fish:** rays, skates, and sharks make up this group.

**Jawless fish:** only hagfish and lampreys fall into this small group.

Pyjama cardinalfish

A bony fish has a skeleton with a skull, ribs, and a backbone.

Fish skin is slimy and covered in scales to protect it from damage.

The gills lie behind the eyes.

Fish have fins that keep them upright when they swim.

The tail of a fish sweeps from side to side to push the fish forward.

Mudskipper

## Gills
Like other animals, fish need to take in oxygen to live. But, unlike us, they can breathe underwater using their gills. Fish gulp in water and their gills filter the oxygen out of it.

## Fish out of water
Mudskippers are one of the few kinds of fish that can survive out of water. They have special gills that take oxygen from air or water. They skip along mudflats using their fins as elbows.

Which fish is the slowest in the ocean?

## The art of swimming

Many fish swim like snakes slide—they wriggle in an "S" shape. Their whole bodies move from side to side and their tails flick to push them forward. Their fins help to steer them.

## Scales

Most fish are covered in hundreds of scales, which overlap like roof tiles. Tiny animals can get under the scales and harm the fish, so they let other animals clean them regularly.

Mandarin fish

Colors can be used for camouflage or to attract a mate.

Some fish can turn on their sides and roll all the way over. A few even swim upside down!

Carp

## Color

Fish come in all colors and patterns. Freshwater fish and those living in cool waters tend to be dull in color. Tropical fish are sometimes incredibly bright and beautiful.

Eels are found in freshwater and saltwater.

## Living together

Fish sometimes live in huge groups called schools. When so many swim together they look like one big fish, so they are less likely to be attacked.

## Fishy features

Most fish look like the pyjama cardinalfish on the left. Some, however, have a different appearance. This eel looks more like a snake with fins. Like a snake, it has sharp teeth.

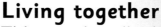

The seahorse is the slowest fish that lives in the ocean.

# Finding food

Most fish are meat-eaters, which means everyone is eating everyone in the water. It's a very dangerous place!

### Electric eel

This eel has three electric organs in its body. It catches prey by giving them electric shocks. These can stun or kill a fish and send a human to the hospital!

## Fish eat fish

The ocean is one great big food chain. Tiny plankton are eaten by small fish and big fish eat the smaller ones.

**Plankton:** plankton contains tiny creatures that live near the surface.

**Herring:** small fish like herring like to eat the tiny plankton.

**Salmon:** larger fish, such as salmon, eat the smaller fish, and they get eaten by sharks!

### Catching prey

Some fish, such as the pike, lie in wait for their meal to swim past. Others are active hunters who chase fast-moving fish through the water.

Pike

### Parrot fish

Parrot fish have a "beak" like a parrot's, which is made from teeth. They use it to gnaw at the coral they eat.

Which fish has extra teeth?

Fish are attracted to the glowing bait that sits right by its mouth.

## The angler fish
A deepwater angler does what fishermen do. Attached to its head is a glowing "rod and bait" that attracts small fish. When one of them gets close, it gets gobbled up!

Archerfish can snap insects out of the air.

Archerfish

**Turn and learn**
Ultimate meat-eaters of the sea—sharks: **pp. 152-153**

## Archerfish
Most fish feed in water, but a few can catch food out of water too. The archerfish shoots water at insects, making them fall into the water, and then it eats them. It can also leap in the air and pick insects off branches.

An experienced adult can shoot out a jet of water four times its own length.

## Piranhas
Piranhas have a fearsome reputation. Their razor-sharp teeth can strip the flesh from animals in minutes. Piranhas eat fruit and seeds as well as animals.

Piranhas work in groups to tear creatures to pieces.

Piranhas

It is extremely dangerous for animals, humans included, to swim in water filled with piranhas.

147

The deep-sea viperfish has extra teeth in its throat to help push its food down.

# Staying alive

So many water creatures feed on fish that they all have to be careful—or very cunning—to make sure they don't get eaten.

Porcupine fish

The flat porcupine fish usually looks like any other fish in the tropical seas.

## Ballooning up

The porcupine fish seems harmless until it is scared. It then gulps in water to blow itself up, which pushes out its spines, making it impossible to swallow.

## Safety in numbers

Fish that live in schools, or groups, are far safer in large numbers. They all keep an eye out for enemies and will sometimes split into two groups to confuse them.

## Camouflage

Many fish use camouflage to hide. Flatfish, such as this plaice, bury themselves on the seafloor, then change their color to blend into the sand and the stones.

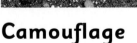
What is the most poisonous fish in the world for a human to eat?

The bright stripes on a lionfish warn other creatures off: the venom in its fins can be deadly.

Twinspot wrasse

Lionfish

## The con artist
The twinspot wrasse tries to fool its enemies. There are two big spots on its body that look like eyes. It buries itself in the sand and just shows the spots, making it look like a large, frightening fish.

## Friend or foe?
These clownfish use venomous sea anemones for protection; the venom doesn't seem to affect the fish, who dive in when danger approaches.

## Venom
The bright coloring of some venomous fish tells the predators that they would not make a tasty meal. This spiked lionfish is one of the most venomous fish in the sea.

Clownfish

**Turn and learn**
Insect defense:
pp. 114-115

## Hidey holes
Garden eels dig holes in the sand. During the day they hang out looking like a field of sea grass catching small fish. When threatened they dive back into their holes.

The pufferfish.

# Making more fish

Most fish don't make very good parents—they lay their eggs in the water and abandon them, leaving their young to fend for themselves. Some, however, do stick around.

Baby sticklebacks

## Courting
Some male fish make more of an effort to attract a female than others. The male stickleback builds a nest, then his belly turns red to attract his mate.

The male stickleback guards his eggs until they hatch.

## Millions of eggs
Most fish lay eggs. Perch, like many other fish, lay an enormous number in the hope that some will hatch. Because other fish like to eat the eggs, most will be lost.

## Not a bad dad
The bullhead male is a good parent. The female lays only a few hundred eggs and the male guards them fiercely until they hatch.

## Hatching
Most fish hatch into tiny larvae—fish that are not fully formed. They gradually grow a skeleton, fins, and organs. At this small stage, they can't protect themselves.

Which fish lays the most eggs?

When the male wants to eat, he spits out the eggs.

**Turn and learn**
Other animals that lay eggs in the water: **pp. 98-99**

## The ultimate protection

The yellowhead jawfish father has a foolproof way to protect his eggs. After the female has laid them, he keeps them inside his mouth until they hatch.

The father seahorse keeps the babies inside his pouch until they can defend themselves.

Seahorses

## Seahorses

The seahorse is very unusual indeed—the female lays the eggs inside a pouch on the male's belly and then the male gives birth to the babies!

A seahorse keeps itself in one position by wrapping its tail around a plant.

## The incredible journey

Some fish have a special place where they lay their eggs. A salmon lives in the sea but travels as far as 1,000 miles (1,500 km) up rivers to lay its eggs in the same place it was born. It even swims up waterfalls to get there.

151

The ocean sunfish can lay a staggering 30 million eggs at once.

## Shark types

There are many different types of shark. Some look very different from the common torpedo shape.

**Leopard shark:** it has golden spotted skin that camouflages it well.

**Saw shark:** its long nose has razor-sharp teeth down it, like a saw.

**Hammerhead:** this shark has a rectangular head with eyes at each end.

**Wobbegong:** it has weedy flaps around its nose for camouflage.

# Sharks and rays

A shark's fin poking out of the water is enough to send a chill down your spine. But they also fill fish with fear—sharks are the largest and most successful meat-eaters in the sea.

## Bendy bodies

Sharks and rays do not have bones. Instead, their skeletons are made of soft, flexible cartilage—the same stuff that's in your nose and ears.

Black-tipped reef shark

Many people think that great whites are the most dangerous animals in the sea, but they rarely attack humans.

Great white shark

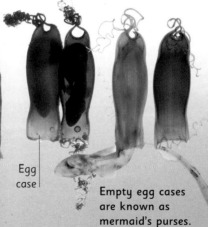

Egg case

Empty egg cases are known as mermaid's purses.

## Born in a purse

Some sharks start life as a tiny baby in an egg case, which looks a bit like a handbag. This case is attached to seaweed and the baby shark grows inside for about six to nine months.

## A lethal smile

The massive jaws of the great white shark contain a terrifying set of sharp teeth, which often fall out as they tear flesh. A shark may lose 30,000 teeth in a lifetime. They are, however, always replaced with new ones.

What is the largest fish in the world?

## The gentle giant

Although all sharks eat meat, not all of them eat big prey. This basking shark is an underwater giant but eats only the tiniest creatures. It gulps huge amounts of water and filters tiny animal plankton from it.

Rays' mouths are on the underside of their bodies. They have strong teeth for crushing shells.

## Rays

Rays are sharks' cousins, but unlike their relatives, they are flat and live mostly on the seabed in shallow, warm water.

Rays swim by flapping their side fins just like wings.

Spotted ray

### Turn and learn

Large sea animals that feed by filtering tiny animals:
**pp. 46-47**

## Up to their eyeballs

Most rays are colored to match the seabed, but they also burrow into the sand for extra camouflage. When they rest, blue spotted stingrays bury themselves with just their eyes showing.

Some rays, such as stingrays, have spines on their tails that can sting predators.

## Monster of the deep

The manta ray is the monster in the family, sometimes stretching 20 ft (6 m) across—that's almost the length of a bus! Some swim in small schools, but most live alone.

The whale shark is the biggest fish in the world.

# Amazing animal facts

The mosquito is the most dangerous animal on Earth to humans. It carries deadly diseases such as malaria.

Malaria kills up to 2 million people every year.

## Reptiles and amphibians

This section can claim the oldest animals in the world, and some of the most venomous too.

**Largest reptile:** the saltwater crocodile can be up to 23 ft (7 m) long.

**Oldest reptile:** there has been one tortoise who lived for 150 years!

**Deadliest snake:** the carpet viper is responsible for the most human deaths.

**Largest toad:** the cane toad would sit happily on a dinner plate—and fill it.

**Largest amphibian:** the giant salamander is as big as an average man.

## Mammals

The mammal section includes the largest, loudest, and tallest animals in the world.

**Largest land animal:** the African bush elephant is the largest land animal.

**Smallest land mammal:** the pygmy white-toothed shrew is the smallest land mammal in the world.

**Loudest land animal:** the loudest land animal is the howler monkey.

**Tallest animal:** the tallest animal on Earth is the giraffe.

## Birds

The bird section contains the incredible record breakers of the flying world.

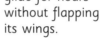

**Largest wingspan:** an albatross can glide for hours without flapping its wings.

**Smallest bird:** the tiniest bird is the bee hummingbird.

**Fastest diver:** the fastest air diver is the peregrine falcon.

**Largest bird:** the largest bird in the world is the ostrich.

The cheetah is the...

What is the rarest large land mammal in the world?

## Creepy-crawlies

The creepy-crawly section contains some of the most extraordinary-looking animals on Earth.

**Largest moth:** The atlas moth is often mistaken for a bird. It is 12 in (30 cm) wide.

**Biggest eye:** the giant squid has the largest eye of any living animal.

**Largest spider:** the Goliath bird-eating spider would easily cover a plate.

**Most legs:** the animal with the most legs is the millipede—some have 750!

The three-toed sloth of South America is the slowest mammal on Earth.

This sloth has an average ground speed of 6½ ft (2 m) per minute. But in the trees it can double that speed.

## Fish

Fish dominate the water world—and the majority of the Earth is covered in water.

**Most fish eggs:** the ocean sunfish can lay 30 million eggs at one spawning.

**Largest fish:** the whale shark is the largest fish in the world.

**Largest freshwater fish:** the European catfish is the largest freshwater fish.

**Prickliest fish:** in addition to spines, porcupine fish also have sharp teeth.

**Fastest fish:** the sailfish can swim faster than the cheetah can run (see below).

...fastest-running animal on Earth.

Cheetahs run amazingly fast. When they are chasing prey on level ground, they can reach speeds of over 60 mph (100 kph) in short bursts.

The Javan rhinoceros, of which there are fewer than 60 left.

# True or false?

Can you figure out which of these facts are real, and which are completely made up?

2 Snakes use their tongues to smell.

1 The brown bear is the largest bear.

3 Most penguins live in the Arctic.

5. False—it is the tallest 6. True 7. False—the males have the pouch 8. True

4 Hummingbirds can fly backward.

5 The giraffe is the world's second-tallest animal.

6 Butterflies rest with their wings closed.

7 Female seahorses have a pouch where they keep their eggs.

8 Tortoises lived among the dinosaurs.

157

Answers: 1. False—it is the polar bear 2. True 3. False—most live in the Antarctic 4. True

# Quiz

Test your knowledge of animals with these tricky quiz questions.

**5** Where do tigers live?

A: Africa          B: North America
C: South America   D: Asia

**1** What is a group of lions called?

A: Troop          B: Pride
C: Clan           D: Pack

**2** How many pairs of legs does an insect have?

A: 2              B: 3
C: 4              D: 5

**6** What are vultures famous for?

A: Digging        B: Growling
C: Scavenging     D: Dancing

**3** What type of bear is this?

A: American black  B: Spectacled
C: Sun             D: Brown

**7** Snakes don't have...

A: Teeth          B: Tongues
C: Eyelids        D: Nostrils

**4** Which member of the parrot family cannot fly?

A: Pileated parrot B: Kakapo
C: Blue lorikeet   D: Brown lory

**8** How many legs does an octopus have?

A: 6  B: 7
C: 8  D: 9

**9** Mammals that carry their young in pouches are called...

A: Marsupials  B: Primates
C: Monotremes  D: Rodents

**10** How many toes do ostriches have on each foot?

A: 2  B: 3
C: 1  D: 5

**11** What is the loudest land animal on Earth?

A: Howler monkey  B: Gorilla
C: Orangutan  D: Baboon

**12** I am an arachnid. What could I be?

A: Frog  B: Spider
C: Crab  D: Insect

**13** How long have fish lived on Earth?

A: 200 million years  B: 300 million years
C: 400 million years  D: 500 million years

**14** A juvenile frog is called a...

A: Nymph  B: Tadpole
C: Maggot  D: Kitten

**15** How long can a hippo hold its breath?

A: 2 minutes  B: 3 minutes
C: 4 minutes  D: 5 minutes

**16** I am the world's largest fish. What am I?

A: Sunfish  B: Basking shark
C: Manta ray  D: Whale shark

**17** Which bird has the longest wingspan?

A: Albatross  B: Golden eagle
C: Ostrich  D: Andean condor

# Who am I?

Can you figure out which animal is being described from the clue?

Orangutan

**2:** I am one of the only animals to use tools.

Great blue heron

Flamingo

Pileated gibbon

Marabou stork

**1:** My feathers are dyed pink by the shrimp I eat.

Komodo dragon

Painted stork

Gray crowned crane

Green iguana

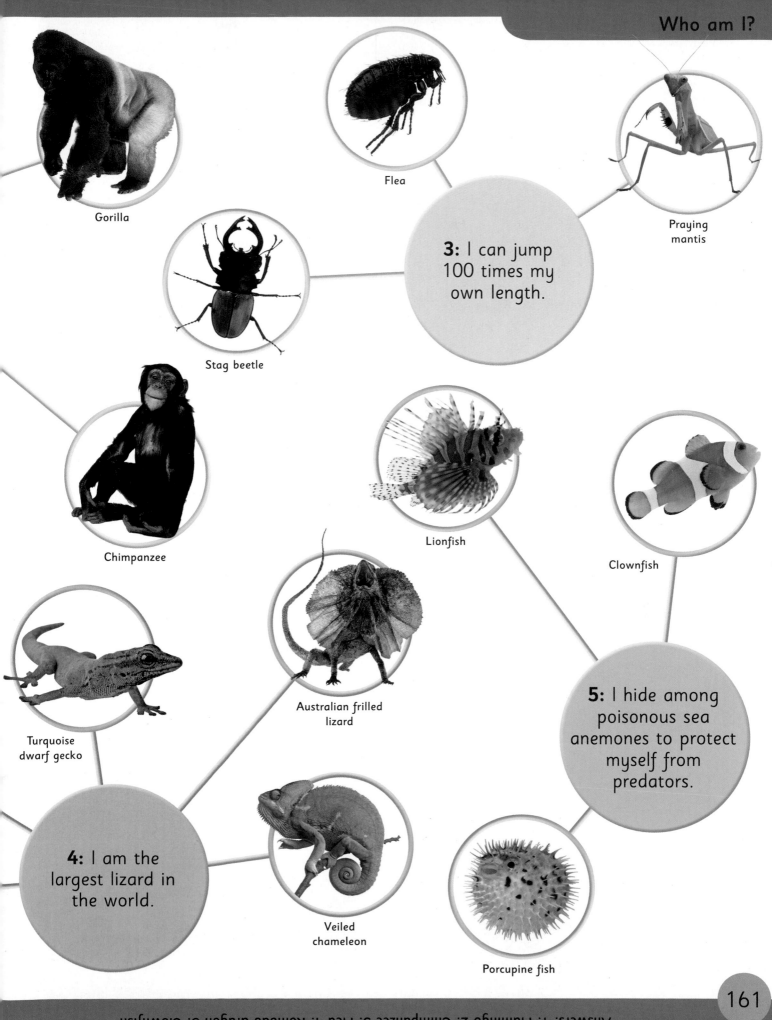

Gorilla

Flea

Praying mantis

Stag beetle

**3:** I can jump 100 times my own length.

Chimpanzee

Lionfish

Clownfish

Turquoise dwarf gecko

Australian frilled lizard

**5:** I hide among poisonous sea anemones to protect myself from predators.

**4:** I am the largest lizard in the world.

Veiled chameleon

Porcupine fish

**2:** This animal, which lives in the Arctic Circle, can hold its breath for up to two minutes underwater.

**3:** This legless Eurasian lizard looks like a snake, but it has eyelids and its tongue is not forked.

**1:** Every winter this animal travels all the way from cold Canada to warm Mexico.

**5:** This North African animal has two toes that are widely spaced for walking on sand.

**8:** This Amazonian animal is brightly colored to warn off predators.

# Where in the world?

Discover where each animal lives by matching the descriptions with the pictures.

**9:** This Antarctic animal is specially camouflaged to make it hard to see underwater.

Camel     Slow worm     Great white shark     Polar bear     Tuatara     Koala

162

**4:** This Asian animal eats bamboo shoots.

**7:** This underwater hunter may lose 30,000 teeth in a lifetime.

**6:** This Asian animal hides from predators among plants.

**10:** This African animal hunts animals that come down to the water's edge to drink.

**12:** This New Zealand animal can live for more than 100 years.

**11:** This Australian animal eats eucalyptus leaves and sleeps for up to 19 hours a day.

Crocodile

Giant panda

Monarch butterfly

Orchid mantis

Penguin

Poison dart frog

Answers. 1: Monarch butterfly 2: Polar bear 3: Slow worm 4: Giant panda 5: Camel 6: Orchid mantis

# Glossary

**abdomen** Rear part of the body of an insect, spider, or crustacean

**amphibian** Animal that can live in and out of water

**antennae** Pair of long, thin feelers on the heads of insects and some non-insects

**arachnid** Animal with simple eyes and eight legs, such as a spider or scorpion

**bacteria** Group of tiny living organisms with just one cell

**baleen** Brushlike fringe in the mouths of certain whales. It is used to strain plankton out of seawater when they eat

**blubber** Thick layer of fat in whales and other sea mammals that helps them stay warm in the water

**breeding** Process by which males and females mate and produce offspring

**camouflage** Colors or patterns on an animal's body that help it blend into its surroundings so it is hidden from view

**carnivore** Animal that mainly eats meat. A lion is a carnivore

**cartilage** Flexible, tough tissue in the skeletons of some animals. A shark's skeleton is made up of only cartilage

**compound eyes** Type of eye that has many light-sensitive surfaces. Each surface sees part of an image. Most adult insects have compound eyes

**courtship** Way in which animals behave to find and attract a partner for mating

**crustacean** Invertebrate, such as a crab or lobster, that has two antennae or feelers and a hard outer body. This group lives mostly in water

**droppings** Waste produced by animals such as insects, rodents, or birds

**extinct** Describes a species that has no living members

**habitat** Place where an animal naturally lives or grows

**herbivore** Animal that only feeds on plants. Cattle are herbivores

**hibernation** When animals, such as bats, sleep throughout winter, when food is scarce

**invertebrate** Animal, such as an earthworm, that does not have a backbone

**larva** Young form that hatches out of the eggs of insects. They usually look very different from their parents. For example, a caterpillar becomes a butterfly

**mammal** Warm-blooded animal whose body is covered in fur (or hair) and who produces milk to feed its young

**marsupial** Type of mammal whose females have pouches to carry their young

**metamorphosis** Major change that happens to the bodies of certain animals as they grow from babies to adults. Tadpoles turn into frogs through metamorphosis

**migration** Long-distance, seasonal journey made by some animals to find food, warmer weather, or to breed

**mollusk** Invertebrate that has a soft body without any divided parts, often covered by a shell. A snail is a mollusk

**non-insect** Any invertebrate that is not an insect, such as starfish, centipedes, and worms

**parasite** Animal that lives on or inside another species to feed off it

**plankton** Tiny creatures that live in water in huge numbers. They serve as food for sea animals

**predator** Animal that hunts other animals for food

**primate** Mammals that have hands and feet that can grasp, a large brain, and good vision. Gorillas are primates

**reptile** Cold-blooded animals that breathe through lungs, usually lay eggs, and are covered with scales or bony plates. Snakes are reptiles

**scales** Thin, flat, and hard plates that cover the bodies of certain animals, such as reptiles and fish

**scavenger** Animal, such as a hyena or vulture, that feeds on the remains of dead animals

**school** Large number of fish swimming together

**species** Type of living thing that can breed with others of the same type

**thorax** Middle part of an insect's body to which the wings and legs are attached

**venomous** Describes animals that use poisonous fangs or stings to kill or paralyze their prey and enemies

**vertebrate** An animal that has a backbone and an internal skeleton

# Index

# Picture credits

**The publisher would like to thank the following for their kind permission to reproduce their photographs:**

(Key: a-above; c-center; b-below; l-left; r-right; t-top)

**Alamy Images**: Photo 24/Brand X Pictures 12tl; Byron Schumaker 121r; D. Robert Franz/Imagestate 18br; Esa Hiltula 19cl; Focus Group/Lynne Siler 42cr; Marin Harvey 12b; Mark Hamblin 19tl; Mark J. Barrett 40l; Maximilian Weinzierl 121ca; Mohamad Haghani 83cra; Paul Horsted/Stock Connection, Inc 91cbr; Steve Bloom Images 13r; Tom Brakefield/Stock Connection Inc 32-33b. **Ardea London Ltd**: 53tc; Becca Saunders 152claa; Chris Knights 69crb, 74clb; D. Parer & E. Parer-Cook 46tr; Donald D. Burgess 55tr; G. Robertson 66tr, 67tr; Jean Paul Ferrero 41tr, 133tr, 134-135cb; Joanna Van Gruisen 154cr; John Cancalosi 54br; Kenneth W. Fink 13b, 21clb, 72bl; M. Watson 54tr, 95cla; Pat Morris 25tr, 97cr, 124tr, 146ca; Peter Steyn 87cr; Stefan Meyers 52-53b; Steve Hopkin 115tl; Valerie Taylor 139c, 146cr, 155cb. **Corbis**: 72-73bc; Anthony Bannister; Gallo Images 107c, 130cr, 150br; Bohemian Nomad Picturemakers 155br; Bryan Knox; Papilio 123bl; Buddy Mays 155br; Carol Hughes; Gallo Images 106b; Chase Swift 37c; Chinch Gryniewicz; Ecoscene 131t; D. Robert & Lorri Franz 9tr; Dan Guravich 119tc; David A. Northcott 154-155b; Douglas Faulkner 44-45c; Douglas P. Wilson; Frank Lane Picture Agency 140tr, 141tl, 141cr; Fritz Polking; Frank Lane Picture Agency 113clb; Galen Rowell 9r; George D. Lepp 118br; Herb Watson 4cla; Joe McDonald 9bc, 30tl, 99tr; Karl Ammann 41cl; Kennan Ward 46crb; Kevin Schafer 10tr; Lynda Richardson 123cb; Martin Harvey 33br, 85cr; Mary Ann McDonald 22tl; Michael & Patricia Fogden 52cl, 94tr; Paul A. Souders 51cr, 124-125b; Paul Funston; Gallo Images 106cl; Peter Johnson 124cl; Tim Davis 21tr; Tom Nebbia 78-79b; W. Perry Conway 28br, 29tr, 33t; Wolfgang Kaehler 53cr, 53bl, 79cr. **Dorling Kindersley**: Andy Crawford and Kit Houghton 36tr; Barnabas Kindersley 64bl; Barrie Watts 29bl, 56bl; Franklin Park Zoo 8ca; Gables 68cr; Jane Burton 61bc; Jerry Young 53tl, 63tc, 63crb, 64bc, 74-75bc, 76crbb, 79cl, 80cbl, 84clb, 85cla, 85cl, 101clb, 101cb, 110cr, 130tl, 130bl, 143tc; Kim Taylor 58cr; Mike Linley 100cr; NASA 70tc; Natural History Museum 4r, 47craa, 50bcl, cbl, 51clb, 55bc, bccr, bcr, 55cla, claa, 71cb, 74bc, 84cl, 118tr, 118cra, 118cl, 118car, 118cbl, 120crb,

121clb, 121bl, 135tr; Paignton Zoo 39tc; Paradise Park Cornwall 78tr; Philip Dowell 79tr; Philip Enticknap 76crb; University College 8tl; Weymouth Sea Life Center 139cl; Jerry Young / Jerry Young 162bc, Philip Dowell / Philip Dowell 162bl, Natural History Museum, London 163bc, 164tr, Rollin Verlinde 154cl. **Getty Images**: Cousteau Society 145cbr; David Nardini 148l; Douglas D. Seifert 153b; Georgette Douwma 145r; JH Pete Carmichael 91t; John Downer 35br; Natalie Fobes 151bl; Peter David 147tl; Tim Davis 66l; Frank Krahmer / Photographer's Choice RF 163fbr. **Dreamstime.com**: Dragoneye 157l, Eric Isselee 161tr, Isselee 51br, 163br, Saskia Massink / Saspartout 119cra, Peter Leahy / Pipehorse 165br. **Fotolia**: Eric Isselee 158tr, 160cr, 162br, 163bl; **Robert Harding Picture Library**: 92ca. **Image Quest Marine**: Carlos Villoch 151tl; James D. Watt 138l, 152cla; Nat Sumanatemeya 135tl; Scott Tuason 138cr. **FLPA - Images of Nature**: David Hosking 63tr; G Moon 77cl; Mike Jones 57clb; Minden Pictures 64cl, 64br, 77t; S. Charlie Brown 61clb; S Maslowski 62bl; Steve Young 65cl. **Masterfile UK:** Albert Normandin 40-41b. **National Geographic Image Collection**: Bill Curtsinger 84c; J. Eastcott/Y.Eastcott Film 20cr; Raymond Gehman 94bl; Robert Madden 59cl; Roy Toft 20-21b; Tim Laman 101r. **Nature Picture Library Ltd**: Alan James 153tl; Anup Shah 95br; Brandon Cole 152bl; Bruce Davidson 120c; Conrad Mauf 89c; Dan Burton 133tl; Fabio Liverani 103cr; Georgette Douwma 145tl; Jurgen Freund 91clb; Pat de la Harpe 95tr. **N.H.P.A.**: Andy Rouse 9clbb, 16cr, 17tl, 17cl, 36crb, 46-47b; Ann & Steve Toon 16bl, 23br; Ant Photo Library 33cb, 125br; Anthony Bannister 24-25, 92-93cb, 111tr; B Jones & M Shimlock 47bc, 149bl; Christophe Ratier 78cr; Dan Griggs 114cb; Daniel Heuclin 26tr, 27c, 32tr, 96cra, 97crb, 154br; David & Irene Myers 46cl; E A Janes 39bl; Eric Soder 14l; G.I Bernard 116crb; Gerard Lacz 23clb, 45bl; Hellio & Van Ingen 37tl, 117tl; Henry Ausloos 18bl; J & A Scott 9tl,

16-17b, 38ca; James Warwick 70cr; Jany Sauvanet 26bl, 147clb; John Buckingham 98bc; John Shaw 14bc, 23bl, 75br; Karl Switak 90cl; Kevin Schafer 11tr, 54, 67b; Laurie Campbell 65r, 82bl; LUTRA 146bl, 150cla; Manfred Danegger 24bc; Marin Wendler 15br; Mark Bowler 42tr; Martin Harvey 15bl, 34cl; Martin Wendler 93clb; Melvin Grey 57r; Mirko Stelzner 73r; Nick Garbutt 10bl, 36bl; Norbert Wu 45tr; Rich Kirchner 67c; Rod Planck 117b; Roger Tidman 31t; Stephen Dalton 11br, 23clbb, 30br, 30-31c, 31br, 60br, 61cr, 71t, 87tl, 87clb, 101tl, 103bl, 120bl, 122l, 126-127b, 130cra, 131br; Stephen Krasemann 43cl; T Kitchin & V Hurst 22tr. **Oxford Scientific Films**: 35tc, 113br, 131c; Adam Jones 62-63b; Alan Root/SAL 26crb; Bert & Babs Wells 32cra; Bob Bennett 39cla; Brian Kenney 13tl, 112tr; Carol Farneti Foster 14cra; Clive Bromhall 13c; Daniel Cox 18tl, 65tl; F. Polking/OKAPIA 62bc; Frank Schneidermeyer 15tr; James H Robinson 112br; Javed Jaffeji 23ca; John Downer 76-77b; John Forsdyke 116br; Jorge Sierra Antinolo 10c; Judd Cooney 77cb; Kim Kesterskov 64t, 154c; Leonard Lee Rue 11tl; Lon E Lauber 76cra; London Scientific Films 108l; Mark Hamblin 37bl, 65br; Michael Dick/AA 10cr; Michael Fogden 60c, 89bl; Michael H. Francis/OKAPIA 40crb; Mike Powles 43cr; Paolo Fioratti 39clbb; Paulo de Oliveira 36cla; Peter Hawkey/SAL 76ca; Richard Packwood 38tr; Rob Nunnington 39tr; Robert Tyrell 60bl, 154cb; Roger Brown 32cr; Satoschi Kuribayashi 121tl; Stan Osolinski 11bl, 37cr, 38-39b, 42c; Thomas Haider 44l; Tom Ulrich 39clb, 39claa; Wendy Shattil and Bob Rozinski 23tl; Zig Leszczynski/AA 47tl. **Science Photo Library**: 140cr, 140bl; Dr Tony Brain 141bl; Eye of Science 127c, 141br; Rod Planck 25bl. **Still Pictures**: James Gerholdt 99cr; Klein 32c; Martin Harvey 42-43b.

**All other images © Dorling Kindersley www.dkimages.com**

## Acknowledgments

**Dorling Kindersley would like to thank:** Ben Morgan for his extensive knowledge on the subject, Lynn Bresler for compiling the index, Lorrie Mack for proofreading, and Janet Allis, Cathy Chesson, Jacqueline Gooden, and Cheryl Telfer for design assistance.